THOUGHT CATALOG BOOKS

The Real Shark's Tank

The Real Shark's Tank

The Truth About Online Dating for Women

L.V. KRAUSE

Thought Catalog Books

Brooklyn, NY

THOUGHT CATALOG BOOKS

Copyright © 2016 by L.V. Krause

All rights reserved. Published by Thought Catalog Books, a division of The Thought & Expression Co., Williamsburg, Brooklyn. Founded in 2010, Thought Catalog is a website and imprint dedicated to your ideas and stories. We publish fiction and non-fiction from emerging and established writers across all genres. For general information and submissions: manuscripts@thoughtcatalog.com.

Second print edition, 2016
ISBN 978-0692698532
10 9 8 7 6 5 4 3 2 1

Cover photography by © Shutterstock.com/Netfalls-Remy Musser

Contents

Introduction

Can you meet someone great through online dating? Of course you can. Many have. But your journey to love will likely be traveled over mountainous land, and some mud, too. It's like a long, torturously extended version of *The Bachelor*, except you don't get to travel to any exotic locations, or be on TV, either. I got so fed up with the entire process I was ready to get a tattoo on my face, just like Mike Tyson, and be done with it.

So how did I cope? In a variety of ways. One night, after one or two, or maybe it was three glasses of deliciously chilled Pinot Grigio, I changed my search function on Match to search for women. To be clear, I wasn't changing teams. I simply decided that online dating was so trying that I needed my own personal Samantha, Carrie, Miranda, and Charlotte to help me through. I didn't know which of the *Sex and the City* women I was most like (yes, I did), or if Match would kick me off for messaging other women, but I was ready to find out.

I found a supportive group of girlfriends who made online dating a little—okay, a lot—more fun. As one of my dates jokingly complained, "You're unionizing!"

Later in my online dating sojourn, I decided to try to figure out what it was about online dating that made it such a perfect storm of bad dates and disappointment. Some of what I discovered, the online dating execs do not want you to know. (Like the lopsided percentages of women versus men on the online dating websites, and what scientists think of all those magical matching formulas.)

And I uncovered fascinating research about what makes players tick, how to avoid them, and why the online dating websites are their personal safari kingdoms.

The Real Shark's Tank was written for every woman who's ever online dated, except for the two women in the United States who found love on their first online date.

I enjoyed writing it more than I did the dates.

1

Wine Pairs Well With Oreos

"All sorrows can be borne if you put them in a story
or tell a story about them."
–Karen Blixen

"Insanity: Doing the same thing over and over
again and expecting different results."
–Albert Einstein

I was awake at three in the morning, having one of those restless nights where you wonder why you even bothered to go to bed. I was mulling the recent promising correspondence I'd started with a man on Match.com. We'd discovered after an email or two that our grandfathers' farms—on the other side of the country from where we now lived—had been less than a hundred miles apart. And he'd closed his last email with a few lines by a poem by Pablo Neruda, a South American poet known for his passionate poems.

Pablo Neruda! Even my hardened heart was glowing a little. I reached for my phone and did a middle of the night email check, hoping for yet another message from the man who liked poetry.

I was in luck! I sat up and started to read his short message. He'd answered a question I'd asked about his grandfather's farm, and then attached a link he said he thought I would enjoy.

Expecting something like a photo of a silo in the setting sun or maybe a picturesque barn, I clicked on the link. It was a video of a very pretty blonde woman sitting on a sofa. She smiled and started to talk about the merits of sex with elves, who in Iceland are not short, grizzled gnomes, but rather tantalizing and tall sexual creatures.

Yep, in Iceland, sometimes people fantasize about having sex with elves. Or maybe in Iceland they really do have sex with elves, I mean, stranger things have happened, but the point was that my latest Match beau had just sent me a link to a site where a woman prattled on quite enthusiastically about elves' magnificent sexual capacities, and their "shimmering sperm." Icelandic elves are apparently also fantastic at oral sex and have "incredible tongues." I abandoned sleep and headed downstairs for a bag of Double Stuf Oreos and some milk.

I sat down at my kitchen table in front of my laptop and watched the video link again. I'd missed a few points on the first watching. The blonde Icelandic woman warned against trying a golden shower with an elf, because they're not like us, and it can really sting.

I stood up, went to the refrigerator, and poured myself a glass of Chardonnay. I sat back down and sipped the smooth wine, which paired surprisingly well with the Oreos.

What was the deal with online dating, anyway? For all the

gauzy TV ads and the money and time spent, none of my girlfriends had established a lasting relationship from online dating.

My mind wandered back to my first online date. I'd joined a dating website and barely five minutes later I'd been instant messaged by a nice-looking man who'd suggested meeting at a popular, local bar. I'd impulsively agreed and hopped into my car. (After three changes of clothes and a subtle black cat-eye eyeliner application.)

As I walked up to the bar, a man who looked like a much older version of his photo waved me over. I already needed a drink so I quickly agreed to his suggestion that we order up a couple of margaritas. He told the bartender to bring over the tequila bottle that looked like a penis. The bored-looking bartender brought a bottle of AsomBroso tequila over and sat it on the bar in front of me. He'd obviously heard this before, and perhaps from the same man.

I eyed the tequila bottle. It did look remarkably like a penis, from the balls-like bottom right up to the bottle-stopper head, though the part that was supposed to be like the shaft was really rounded and I'd never seen a penis that looked like that, though I'm not saying there isn't one somewhere.

My date said, "Women line up for these bottles when they're empty." He smiled at me expectantly and I replied, "That's very interesting." In my defense, I'd lived in a Southern city for a number of years and as everyone in the South knows, that's what you say when you're a bit taken aback. Or horrified.

I drank the excellent margarita the bartender mixed up using the penis-bottle tequila and left the bar as soon as I could. The next day I received a sext from Penis Bottle Man, who still seemed captivated by the endless possibilities of a penis-shaped tequila bottle, and we'll leave it at that. My cousin, a jaundiced veteran of the online dating world, told me it was my fault for seeming interested in the penis-tequila bottle. (I wasn't interested! I was being polite!)

I blithely continued online dating, clearly ignoring what was a sign from the Universe. It was like there was a gate in front of a railroad crossing, and I went around it. It was like a tree fell and blocked the road and I climbed over it. It was like—well, you get the idea. I soldiered on.

I sat at my kitchen table with my wine and my Double Stuf Oreos, feeling thoughtful. Online dating had proved to be simultaneously frustrating, time-consuming, and humiliating.

But what was it, *exactly*, that made online dating so awful? Was it that it was a virtual playground for players? Was it the endless bad coffee dates? The men in Alaska leering at our photos and then doing… God knows what?

I finished my glass of wine, feeling a little tipsy. I didn't usually drink in the middle of the night but it really wasn't such a bad idea.

I continued to ponder. Did the magic "matching" algorithms work for anyone?

I didn't know. But I decided to do a little research. It was time to find out:

Was it me, or was it online dating?

2

The All-Important Photo

"It is amazing how complete is the delusion that
beauty is goodness."
–Leo Tolstoy, The Kreutzer Sonata

After my correspondence with Elf Sex Man, I began researching the world of online dating. It turns out that French philosophers are as worried as I about online dating's negative effect on romance. And professors at schools like Northwestern and Duke have been researching the strange new world of online dating, with some disquieting discoveries.

So where to commence our journey into the shortcomings of the online dating world? I think I'll begin with the mind-boggling importance of one's photos.

I don't know about you, but I've had men I've gone on dates with tell me that they almost didn't write me because they didn't like *one* of my photos. I've had men write and recommend that I delete a photo they didn't care for. At one point I just had one primary photo up and men didn't like that, either. (Where was my full body shot? Where?!)

Any woman who's been on Match or OkCupid or POF or eHarmony for more than, say, one day, knows how crucial the primary photo is. It's your key to success in the online dating world. It's your logo, it's your brand, it's the be-all-and-end-all of your online dating life.

I didn't know that, however, when I began online dating. I had my mom take a couple pictures of me standing near their pool. She thought a pair of Ralph Lauren tortoise shell glasses of mine made me look like a cute intellectual, so I put those on and she snapped a couple of shots.

No one has ever stopped me in a shopping mall and asked me to apply to a modeling agency so the pictures looked fine to me. I went home to my apartment and uploaded my photos to my chosen online dating site. Then I wrote a profile that I thought made me sound both fun to be with and willing to discuss whether the Federal Reserve should ease up on their restrictive monetary policies.

When I look back now, I laugh, I scoff, I even tear up a bit, thinking of myself back then: a naïf baby doe, about to tippy-toe into the big, bad world of online dating with a photo of myself in tortoise shell glasses, looking like a cute intellectual.

After I got home from my date with Penis Bottle Man, I got back on the dating website and searched for a kind, intellectual man in my age range. I wrote to a few seemingly good candidates and nobody apparently liked my tortoise shell glasses as much as my mom and so no one responded, though Penis Bottle Man had clearly thought the tortoise shell glasses were rocking.

After my ill-fated date and my lack of responses, I decided that I needed some new photos. I searched through my closet for a pink camera I received as a Christmas gift a few years before that I'd never used because the instructions seemed kind of complicated, and I set out to try to get a better photo.

First, I poured myself a crisp glass of Sauvignon Blanc, and then I read through the camera instructions, including how to use the time delay. I piled a bunch of books on a table to get the camera at the right height, perched the camera precariously on top of the pile, hit the time delay, ran backwards, and tried to look photogenic.

I took photo after photo, feeling increasingly despondent. As all good supermodels know, you need cheekbones to get a good photograph, and my face is, well, cheekbone-less. I kept piling on more eye makeup and changing clothes and the lighting and drinking wine, and finally I hit the time delay on my pink camera, ran backwards and threw myself against a wall, and ended up with a photo that looked—if I do say so myself—kind of seductive. I also looked drunk, which I think is like an elixir to the men on the dating websites. I uploaded my new drunken seductress photo and started getting some emails. Actually, lots of emails.

I had the exact same profile text as when I got practically no emails, but with my new drunk seductress photo, I was being practically deluged with email. And what happened to me was exactly in line with my research.

Academic studies delving into the relationship between physical attractiveness and online dating success have come to the same conclusion that I did after one short day of online dating: if you want to successfully online date, you'd better have a hot photo. I mean, the researchers tactfully call it "a preference for physical attractiveness," but what they mean is: It's a beauty contest without the talent competition.

And, not surprisingly, physical attractiveness is more important to men online than to women. Researchers earnestly delve into how many messages are sent and by whom, using "binary variables" and "linear probability models," and then they conclude exactly what we women already know: men value physical attractiveness above all other traits while online dating.

A California research firm attached something called "Tobii Light Eye Trackers" to laptops in a San Francisco coffee shop and then had male and female café-goers look at Match and eHarmony profiles. They found that the women spent 50 percent longer reading through the profile text than the men, who in turn spent significantly more time gazing at female's photos, rather than the profile text.

Another study, which used data from one of the largest online dating sites, found that the biggest difference between men and women's browsing habits was the significantly higher numbers of profiles that men looked at. Apparently, men *like* to spend hours in front of their computer screens, studying the goods. Which probably explains my emails from Alaska, and Folsom, California, too.

The Profile Matters Not

If you're a "glass-half-full" kind of person, you're probably thinking that men care about our attractiveness, but in the context of all our other wonderful traits… right?

Let's hear what a real life internet dating executive has to say about that. The dating website OkCupid was started in 2004 by four Harvard math majors after they sold their first start-up company, SparkNotes. How they veered from study guides to online dating we'll never know, but I'm sure there's a good story behind it.

One of OkCupid's founders, Christian Rudder, started writing a blog on the website in which he analyzed the data from OkCupid's user base. Here's what he had to say about men messaging attractive women in his blog post "Your Looks and Your Inbox":

> "Site-wide, two-thirds of male messages go to the best-looking third of women. So basically, guys are fighting each other 2-for-1 for the absolute best-rated females, while plenty of potentially charming, even cute, girls go unwritten. The medical term for this is male pattern madness."

You've got to give Christian credit for his refreshing honesty. In yet another blunt post he wrote:

> "We will confront an unfortunate truth of online dating: no matter how much time you spend polishing your profile ... it's your picture that matters most."

Rudder used some of the data gleaned from the OkCupid website to write a best-selling book, *Dataclysm*, for which he earned a 7-figure advance and a thoughtful review in the *Los Angeles Review of Books* questioning his use of unsuspecting OkCupid members for his research.

Rudder emphasized the importance of a woman's photo versus her profile text in yet another OkCupid post in 2014:

"Essentially, the text is less than 10% of what people think of you. So, your picture is worth that fabled thousand words, but your actual words are worth...almost nothing."

I've got to disagree a little with Christian Rudder here, despite his Harvard pedigree. I would occasionally change up my profile a little to see what would happen. For a short period of time, I wrote in my profile that I disliked dogs. And cats, too. I don't dislike dogs and cats but I don't have any pets and let's just leave it at that.

My professed dislike of dogs and cats cut my response level dramatically, thus proving that the profiles do matter, at least a little. I even got a few incensed men writing me. One man went so far as to ask if I'd ever kill a dog (um, no) and another indignantly pointed out his Humane Shelter work while declaring his anger that I had even deigned to write to him.

I often fiddled with my profile and "Dislike both dogs and cats" was quickly discarded from my profile, along with "I don't know what I want in a man, but as Justice Potter Stewart said in his famous Supreme Court decision about pornography, 'I'll know it when I see it.'" (Never mention the word pornography in an online dating profile. You will not be happy with your email results.)

In 2013, OkCupid began offering a for-pay premium feature that allows men, um, I mean all OkCupid members, to filter their searches to view only the top-rated members in terms of physical attractiveness. (OkCupid lets members rate each other on a star scale, though the results are kept private.) For an extra monthly fee, OkCupid members can filter by attractiveness rating and by self-rated body type. One sardonic reporter at CNN.com termed it the "fat" and "ugly" option.

Rudder noted in his OkCupid blog that, "a hot woman receives roughly 4x the messages an average-looking women gets, and 25x as many as an ugly one."

That's just sad. And so is the use of the word "ugly." According to the Global Language Monitor, the English language has approximately 1,025,109 word option choices, and I'd like to propose dropping "ugly" from our repertoire of words forevermore. In fact, I'm thinking of starting a Change.org petition to rid the word "ugly" from the English language. Anyone in for a signature?

I went out on a few dates with a man who had a habit of commenting critically about the looks of the women sitting near us. When he made a disparaging comment about one of my girlfriend's photos on my Facebook page, I finally cut him loose, and then I unfriended him so we didn't have to look at his photo anymore, either.

I've heard it said many times that "men are just more *visual* than women," as if the poor dears just can't help themselves. Here's what I think: men should try *visual-ing* themselves in the mirror in the morning, and then start their day.

Just How Shallow Are Men, Anyway?

A Los Angeles-based female comedy writer named Alli Reed had a delicious idea: she decided to put up a fake profile on OkCupid featuring a super hot photo of a girlfriend of hers, with a horrific profile. In a Cracked.com article, she explained that she wrote, "the OkCupid profile of the Worst Woman on Earth, hoping to prove that there exists an online dating profile so loathsome that no man would message it."

Here's just part of the fake hot girl's fake profile on OkCupid:

You should message me if: ur rich

The most private thing I'm willing to admit: convinced my ex I was pregnant and he still pays me child support   lolololol

On a typical Friday night I am: knockin the cups out of homeless ppls hands its sooooo funny to watch them try to pick it up lolllll"

So, my dear readers, what would you bet, if you had some spare money? Would you put money down that this horrendous fake profile with a super hot photo would be scorned by men for its shallow awfulness?

Nope. In just one day, the fake shitty hot girl received 120 messages. Here's just one of the messages she received:

Man on Okcupid: Hey how's it going? I am ___. What are you doing? Btw you have gorgeous eyes.

Fake hot girl on OKCupid: I'm just pretending to be

a 14 year old on facebook and making fun of some of my sisters friends. LMAOOOO bullying is fun

Man on Okcupid: lol your so funny. hahaha. You a sexy devil lol So dose ur sis know about it? Any plans for the weekend? Btw what's ur number so we can text?"

All I have to say after reading that text exchange is that at least the fake hot girl didn't say she didn't like dogs. Now *that* would have been a test for the ages.

Alli Reed, the comedy writer who conducted the experiment, concluded that she was "confiscating everyone's penis until further notice."

Anorexia is Good

How does a woman's weight affect her online dating success? The research in this area, unfortunately, is just as clear as men's preference for physical attractiveness.

A large study of over 6,000 online daters in San Diego and Boston, which analyzed data from over 800,000 "browsed profile" observations, came to the following sad conclusion: "Men have a strong distaste for women with a large BMI [Body Mass Index], while women tend to prefer heavier men."

And the story gets worse, as it often does when writing about online dating. One of the study's authors commented in an interview that "…it turns out that men care a lot about women's BMI's. In fact, they want women to be slightly anorexic, at like 18-1/2. And you look at women's attractiveness, it goes really up at low BMI and really drops below that."

Perhaps I shouldn't have started this book with the disheartening emphasis men place on physical attractiveness and weight, but any of you who've online dated for more than say, one week, are already aware that a book about online dating isn't going to be a happy fairy tale, but instead a B-grade horror movie in which you are the reluctant star.

You might as well pour yourself your first glass of wine (or another one, if you've already started). There's more where that came from.

3

The Profile-To-Person Disconnect

"Appearances are often deceiving."
–Aesop

It's crazy, if you think about it: the idea that we're going to choose a potential partner after looking at a photo or two and a couple paragraphs of drivel. If you teleported back in time and told a group of 1870s railroad workers in Montana that in the twenty-first century we'd choose our lovers from a catalogue, they'd be astonished. (And if there were an 1870's version of OkCupid the scraggly, toothless railroad workers would still assuredly only write the hottest women.)

So what is it about the idea of choosing from rows of profile photos whom to date and love and perhaps marry that is so fundamentally nuts?

I think it's because of the disconnect between profile and person. I'm not talking about the disconnect between fake ages or old photos, though that's frustrating too. I'm talking about a more fundamental disconnect: the sheer impossibility of getting a real feel about someone from a photo and a short profile description. Or even from a disembodied voice on the telephone.

It's like when you read a funny profile and then you meet the person and he's not funny at all. Or someone's innate kindness doesn't show up in his profile, or his warm smile.

I once read a lovely profile by an English professor who mused that good people often see themselves as bad, and vice versa, which makes other people online virtually unknowable. And, I might add, leads to the utter unreliability of most profiles. Interestingly, a few men have mentioned to me that I seem much sweeter than the impression my profile gives, which may or may not be true.

Dan Ariely, a Duke behavioral economist, turned his academic attention to the online dating world after a new professor moved into an office next to him and started online dating.

According to Ariely's BigThink interview, his male professor friend apparently had a miserable time online dating, which piqued Ariely's interest in examining online dating from an economics perspective. (Why Ariely's professor friend had such a hard time we'll never know, but I'm assuming it wasn't because women sent him obnoxiously sexual first emails, or because the women he met were already having sex with someone else, or because women his own age refused to date him. But I digress.)

Ariely ended up co-authoring a study on online dating in which he posited that online dating isn't working because people are "experience goods" and not "search goods." In other words, people are like craft beer, or perfume. We can't just be ordered up based on objective, dry decision points like you would a flat iron or a blow dryer. (It's so fun writing a book just for women! I don't have to use boring lawnmower examples.)

Ariely and his co-authors compare trying to figure out what someone is like from reading a profile to trying to figure out what a recipe would taste like from studying the list of ingredients. They theorize that there is a "fundamental gap between the kinds of information people both want and need to determine whether someone is a good romantic match and the kind of information available on online dating profiles."

The participants in Ariely's study were asked to list the traits they wanted in a spouse or partner, and experience traits like "makes me laugh," "affectionate," "loyal," "fun," and "gets along with my other friends" ended up being five times more important to daters than the traits typically offered up on dating profiles, like "athletic," "religious," and "physically attractive."

Or your astrological sign, which went out as a dating differentiator in the early 1970's. (Yes, I'm talking to you, Match.)

Writing in *Scientific American,* two prominent psychology researchers suggested, much to my amusement, that online dating might work better if the dating sites offered video sessions. Clearly, the good professors have never online dated, despite their deep interest in the field.

A couple of my girlfriends had men suggest Skype sessions before a first meeting, and a body part somehow always managed to make its way out of the men's pants, almost as if it had a mind of its own.

Bad Date Overload

One big problem with not being able to figure out what a man is like from reading a dating profile is that you may end up going on quite a few bad dates. And online dating can become a real time sucker if you meet too many people in a row who aren't, um, exactly what you had in mind.

I came to the conclusion that coffee dates are kind of like marshmallows. You can start out really liking marshmallows, but after you have fourteen or maybe a hundred bags of them, you just don't really want marshmallows anymore. Maybe ever.

One of my cousins got so fed up with online dating that she took to sending me emails urging me to stop and "taste the sweet nectar of freedom." She had decided that when she was at a Starbucks, she wanted to be the person in front of the laptop secretly listening to the awkward first-date conversation at the table next to her, and not the person answering intrusive questions as to why her past two marriages broke up.

Even a simple coffee date can be a time thief. At a party, if you aren't enjoying talking to someone, you can gradually drift away. When you're on an online date, however, you're stuck with someone for at least forty-five minutes. I know some people can cut coffee dates shorter, but they probably weren't raised in Minnesota. I once met someone at a neighborhood coffee shop, drank my vanilla latte, excused myself to go to the restroom, and came back to find that he'd not only bought me a new latte, but a scone, too. I'd already been there an hour and I don't think I got out of there for another hour, and that's a damn long time to interact with someone you know you're not interested in.

I think my married friends and relatives assume I'm having the time of my life online dating, but really, I'm not.

Ten Questions to Add to the Dating Profiles

One warm spring night, I met my girlfriends for a drink at a bar on Siesta Key. As we sat outside enjoying the breeze off the Gulf, we had a glass or two of wine and then we had some tequila shots and I asked them what kind of information they'd like to see added to the online dating sites, along with politics and religion and pet ownership. The following were some of the admittedly tequila-fueled suggestions:

1. Are you grumpy in the morning? How about at night? Are you grumpy then?
2. What music do you listen to in the car? What is your exact facial expression while listening to music you haven't chosen? Take out your phone. Take a selfie of that expression and upload it.
3. Does your dog or cat sleep with you? When did you last bathe your pet?
4. In your last committed relationship or marriage, did you cheat? If yes, with how many people, you fucking motherfucker?
5. Upon awakening, how long does it take you to get out of bed and brush your teeth? How old is your toothbrush?

6. Do you snore? Buy a decibel meter and measure it. Record that amount.

7. What do you do at night to relax? Can you keep yourself entertained or is that your lucky partner's job?

8. On average, how much porn do you watch weekly? Are you aware that those women are not enjoying being jack hammered?

9. Do you think cellulite is a normal part of a woman's body or do you expect a woman to have thighs like a man's? Or Gisele Bündchen's?

10. How often do you call your mom?

After another Patrón tequila shot or two and some dancing at a club down the street with some Haitian men who seemed to have bodyguards with them for some reason, my girlfriends and I ended the night sleeping on sofas at one of our houses near the beach, none the worse for the wear. A few more questions were added in the early morning hours, but I'll save them for the next book, in which I solve, once and for all, the problem of the space-time continuum.

4

The Expectations Trap

"He had heard that women often love plain ordinary men, but he did not believe it, because he judged himself and he could only love beautiful mysterious exceptional women."
–Leo Tolstoy, *Anna Karenina*

"Men want a runner's body, but without the sun damage."
–My mother

The Farrah Fawcett Effect

I'm cute but no one has ever accused me of being beautiful, which I gradually became convinced was the absolute worst thing to be on an online dating site. Men happily asked me out and dated me but they always thought they could do a little better. Which they probably could. As my beloved mother once observed, my tombstone could read, "She was an acquired taste."

In the online dating world, with its infinity of choices,

there's always someone prettier out there, with better bikini shots (I didn't have any) or larger implants (again, no), just over the horizon. The gorgeous woman on OkCupid or Match who looks just like Miranda Kerr may never write a man back, but her specter hangs over all his interactions.

An older academic study found that college-aged men found normally attractive women much less attractive after watching just a few minutes of *Charlie's Angels*, which featured three of the most beautiful actresses of all time: Farrah Fawcett, Jaclyn Smith and Kate Jackson.

Doug Kenrick, one of the study's authors observed:

> "As in the case of exposure to extremes of water temperature, exposure to extremes of physical appearance affected people's judgments of what was average. As we had predicted, an average-looking woman was judged significantly uglier than normal if the subjects had just been gazing at a series of beauties."

In a follow-up study, men rated their current partners as less desirable after viewing photos in *Playboy* and *Penthouse,* though women didn't view their own partners as less desirable after viewing nude men in *Playgirl*.

Yet another study put a slightly different twist on this unfortunate male tendency, noting that looking at beautiful women's photos reduces men's satisfaction with females "available to the average man."

The problem is, most men don't see themselves as average.

And guess what? Quelle surprise. Studies have shown that, too.

Men Cannot See Themselves

Remember when studies came out with the unsurprising conclusion that a glass of wine a day was good for you? (Already knew it.) And that butter was safe to eat again? (As Julia Child so famously said, "With enough butter, anything is good.")

In yet another study result that will surprise no one, researchers have found that men are unaffected by their own physical attractiveness when choosing whom to message online.

Remember Dan Ariely, the Duke University behavioral economist with the miserable online-dating professor friend? He did another study in which he analyzed data from a site called HOTorNOT.com, where users could rate others as to their hotness, and then message them for dates.

Ariely and his co-authors concluded, among other things:

> "In making date choices, males are less influenced by
> their own rated attractiveness than females are."

A study of a speed-dating event in Germany echoed Ariely's finding. The researchers found that men didn't seem to be influenced by their own desirability, whereas the women at the event chose men who matched them in both physical and social desirability.

No woman who's online dated is surprised to hear this. The academic researchers in this area could save themselves a lot of time and effort and just ask a few female online daters out to lunch sometime. I mean, "Men are less influenced by their own rated attractiveness than females are"? True that. Like you said.

It's not just their own looks that men ignore when choosing whom to message on the online dating sites. Most of us are astonished when men who are completely outside any boundaries we've set nevertheless contact us online. Sometimes, they write a couple times, like maybe we missed the first one.

I've received email from men who looked like they might have wandered into a public library to use the free computers and then decided to open an OkCupid account, listing under their "six favorite things": "Sex, sex, sex, sex, sex, and sex."

My theory for why average-looking men will happily contact only much hotter women is that men's ego strength tends to be stronger than ours, which may be linked to their higher testosterone levels, which is also linked to wars. Who knows? All that's important is it's annoying.

Quit Asking for Triathletes, Dammit

Most men's profiles contain some variation of the following sentence: "While she prefers an old pair of blue jeans and a ponytail, she still loves to dress up and wear a swanky ball gown. Victoria's Secret is under it all."

Most men, of course, aren't going to take you anywhere that would demand a "swanky" ball gown or even a short black cocktail dress, so it's a continuing mystery why "looks good in an evening dress" continues to be a pro forma requirement for women on the dating websites, like having two arms and two legs.

Men seem to assume that the dating websites want them to describe their fantasy woman, though the profile writing instructions say nothing of the kind.

After the generic demand for women who wear tight jeans and long dresses, some men start to pile on the stipulations. They want someone who cooks like Giada De Laurentiis, who competes in triathlons, who is a sensuous vixen, and who will accompany them to their fantasy travel destinations. (On her own dime.)

What men don't seem to understand is that there's not a woman on Earth who's had the time for world travel *and* triathlons *and* cooking like Giada whatever-her-last-name-is. And a woman with an already full life isn't going to subsume herself into a man's hobbies and fantasies.

As a confirmed non-athlete, I was continually frustrated with Floridian men's insistence on female athleticism. (Are the men in Des Moines as activity obsessed? Let me know, and I'll start checking out Craigslist for apartments.) My question is: why can't men just run triathlons on their own? It's not like you can join the men's division and run alongside them.

At one point I even wrote in my profile: "If one more man suggests that we go kayaking, I will move to Chicago, where I assume men will take me to Cubs games and we can drink beer."

This cut down my response level so dramatically—either because the men in Sarasota love to kayak or because it wasn't funny—that I quickly dropped the line, instead going back to my generic generalities about loving "Pilates" (Not really), "hot yoga" (Hell, no), and "volunteering" (maybe next year).

Some men become bizarrely specific in their demands. One man expressed his desire to meet a glamorous woman but who would "pack only a small roll-on suitcase for a trip around the world." One man wanted "a college athlete." Yet another man wrote hopefully: "I'm a good photographer and would like my woman to pose in her favorite swimwear or lingerie."

And this from a man who didn't quite get the online dating world: "She would never go out with someone she met on Match. Unless of course it was me!"

My personal favorite, though, was this: "I'm looking for big breasts, but it's not a deal breaker."

What sort of dating service, exactly, do these men think they joined? One where all their dreams come true?

Sometimes I imagined a man sitting thoughtfully in front of his computer, jiggling the ice in his scotch, before typing: "She should like fly fishing… and swimming naked in a crisp, clear mountain stream." And then I imagined him sitting back in his chair and taking another sip of his scotch, satisfied for the moment with the thought of his perfect woman.

I decided to write the man who requested "a college athlete" to assuage my curiosity about his collegiate-athlete obsession, though the only exercise I got in college was when I took bowling for my required PE class. I asked him if his dates really had to be a former college athlete, and if so, why? He replied, "Not to worry"—as if I were worried—and then asked, as is par for the course in outdoor-activity-obsessed

Sarasota, "What do you do for exercise?" When I replied that I had bowled in college but had since lost my bowling shoes, I never heard from him again, which was, um, fine with me.

Men cannot have it all. And yet the vast illusion of choice gives the impression, however misguided, that a magic princess is out there—a magic princess who runs triathlons—waiting for every man.

I'd Like Her Medium Rare

Some men seem to view the women they meet through the dating websites as items on a menu that can be tweaked to their liking, even after they've met.

A girlfriend of mine drove to Orlando, three hours from Sarasota, to meet a man she'd been enjoying a nice correspondence with, only to have him inform her after their lunch that she needed to wear more make-up. And that she'd look more attractive if she showed more cleavage.

I suggested to her that he might be suffering from early Alzheimer's, like that poor Julianne Moore in *Still Alice*, which was the only logical explanation I could come up with on the spot.

A man whom I met for a drink reached over, ran his hand down my leg, and asked why I was wearing hose, which he didn't like. I politely explained that Kate and Pippa Middleton had brought wearing stockings back into fashion, which shut him up on that subject, but unfortunately not on a few others.

It's time for one of my most embarrassing online dating stories. But if I can make another woman feel better, like I do after seeing photos of movie stars with cellulite in the grocery store check-out line, well, it was all worth it.

One beautiful December night here in Sarasota, I went with an online date to a wine and cheese pre-Christmas party on the grounds of the Ringling Museum. We were standing on a waterfront terrace enjoying a beautiful sunset over the Sarasota Bay. I was drinking a glass of wine and feeling happy and relaxed. I had on a brand-new, chiffon, Elie Tahari shirt and my (problematic) hair had been professionally blown dry. My date turned to me and said, "You're a beautiful woman… "

He paused and knit his brows together.

"… but your teeth need whitening."

He added, quite unnecessarily, since I'd already received the message loud and clear: "They really detract from your looks."

I stared at him, feeling completely deflated. Since I grew up in Minnesota, I thanked him for telling me, and we kept talking about other subjects. I excused myself to go to the bathroom, where I worriedly examined my teeth. Since my face was like six inches away from the bathroom mirror, I felt I had to explain to the other women in the bathroom what I was doing, and why. One of them offered to drive me home on the spot, and no one seemed to think my natural Minnesota reticence had been the optimum way to handle my date's teeth-whitening advice.

I regretfully declined the nice woman's offer of a ride home and returned to my date, who, I may not have previously mentioned, had on a red Christmas sweater with short sleeves. Up to this point in my life, I had been blissfully unaware that they made men's sweaters with short sleeves, but I'm here to tell you that they do.

My Christmas-clad date and I met another couple for dinner, where I quenched my natural inclination to smile and drank perhaps more than the daily recommended wine allowance for women, which I've always thought was too low.

(Five ounces of wine a day? That's like a wine appetizer.)

The next week, at my hastily scheduled teeth-whitening appointment the dental staff assured me that my teeth weren't that bad and that they should know, they saw teeth every day. The entire staff and the very nice dentist were also adamant that I should never see my date again. As one of the dental technicians pointed out, what part of me was he going to criticize next? (I already knew. My upper arms.)

My teeth whitening cost me $525 dollars, which kind of made me mad, but as my mother helpfully pointed out, my teeth did look better.

Beauty is Even More Important Online, if that's Possible

The academicians who study online dating have theorized that one of the reasons men have gotten so picky is because of the seemingly endless numbers of choices on dating websites.

It's puzzling, because it seems so counterintuitive. You'd think that the large membership numbers at Match and OkCupid and POF and eHarmony would ensure that everyone would be able to find a soul mate. Or at least someone to hang out with on Sunday nights to see who gets killed off in the latest episode of *The Walking Dead.*

Given the vast plethora of choice, you'd think that men and women who enjoy brisk early morning walks with their dogs, and men and women who want to drink with the band when the bar closes down, would find each other online.

But it turns out that the massive amount of choices presented on dating websites causes a *more* superficial mindset. And that physical attractiveness becomes *more* important to men online.

Partially, of course, it's a function of how the dating sites work: you're presented with a picture of someone. And you can't hear the photo talk, or laugh, so the photo is pretty much all you have to go on.

But there's more to it than that: what happens is that when faced with a multitude of choices, people often switch into an assessment mentality. What that means is they start to simplify the way they make decisions. They reduce the number of criteria they are using to choose with and get on with it. Dan Ariely pointed out in his BigThink interview that the emphasis on objective criteria while online dating is "exaggerated by the way the system is created."

An influential 2012 study of online dating entitled "Online Dating: A Critical Analysis from the Perspective of Psychological Science" warned that the large membership numbers on the dating websites "cause people to make lazy, ill-advised decisions." The study's co-authors explain the poor decision-making while online dating thusly:

[T]he process of browsing profiles side-by-side is

likely to cause users to overweight features of potential partners that are easy to evaluate via profiles but might be largely irrelevant once a relationship starts to develop … Furthermore, many sites provide users with very large numbers of profiles, causing them to use time-efficient but minimally thoughtful strategies for choosing among them.

So here's how men "use time-efficient but minimally thoughtful strategies for choosing." They write the most attractive women with the most cleavage.

You might be wondering at this point just how many choices it takes, exactly, for things to start getting confusing? One study found that when daters were given 64 online profiles, rather than 24 or 4, they were more likely to reject other daters based on a small number of criteria, like attractiveness and educational standards, rather than viewing others' profiles more holistically.

So at 64 choices things start getting confusing. And how many millions of subscribers do the largest dating sites claim to have? Ten million? Fifteen million? Our brains aren't set up for that.

Researchers have pointed out that the internet has expanded our dating choices "well beyond our processing capacity." In the olden days, people didn't have much choice in their dating options. From what's known of early tribes, people usually hung out with about 150 people. I wouldn't want to go back to those days for a variety of reasons, including the lack of lash-lengthening mascara and mouthwash, but the limitless choices on dating websites are for the birds. (Who, as it turns out, also get confused with too much mate choice, as do frogs.)

5

The Bachelor and The Bachelorette: A Case Study in Choice

Where can you find a selection of attractive singles, primed and ready for love? Well, there's Match and POF and OkCupid and eHarmony… and *The Bachelor* and *The Bachelorette*!

I've watched every season of *The Bachelor* and of *The Bachelorette*, including the very first *Bachelor,* which concluded when Alex the Bachelor chose a woman who smeared his body with chocolate in the fantasy suite instead of the lovely Trista Rehn, astonishing most viewers. Happily, Trista found her handsome fireman Ryan in the first season of *The Bachelorette* and all ended well.

I carved out Monday nights as my *The Bachelor/The Bachelorette* viewing night, and my friends and family knew not to call me during the show. I played my own TV drinking game and took a sip of wine whenever a contestant said the word "journey" or earnestly declared that they were on the show "for the right reasons." (As opposed to personal fame and aggrandizement.)

Some people I know are curious as to why I like watching

The Bachelor and *The Bachelorette* so very, very much. (I'm talking about men. Women don't care what you watch but men seem to think watching anything other than sports and the History Channel signifies a lesser mind.) I usually try to explain that it's like watching a hockey game waiting for a fight, or slowing to get a good look at a traffic accident. It's a disaster in the making, and I can watch from the comfort of my down-cushioned sofa.

Each season starts with the Bachelor or the Bachelorette watching his or her 25 candidates emerge from a steady stream of limos. After an alcohol-fueled cocktail party in which the slightly desperate 25 contestants do various wild, crazy and later deeply embarrassing stunts to catch the Bachelor/Bachelorette's attention, the Bachelor/Bachelorette gives out roses to the lucky 15 or so who've been chosen to stay and fight for the honor of becoming engaged to someone who by the end of the show has most likely slept with at least one other person and in some cases four other people in the weeks before the engagement.

Sometimes, candidates are eliminated because they didn't seem to be on the show "for the right reason." (Drink!) Each episode, more candidates have to go home after the Bachelor/Bachelorette decides to end their "journey." (Drink!) The array of eligible singles initially proves confusing to both the Bachelors and the Bachelorettes as they face the monumental task of judging which man or woman might be their best life mate, given the time constraints and so many choices. And with so much alcohol involved.

Eventually, though, the Bachelor/Bachelorette chooses four candidates for hometown visits with their astonished parents, and then chooses three of those to take (separately) to the fantasy suite, which isn't filmed. (But we occasionally get to hear some sound effects. Yippee.)

On the show's final episode, a "winner" is chosen. If it's a *Bachelorette* season, she chooses which of the two final suitors to marry, leaving one crushed. If it's a *Bachelor* season, he proposes to one woman, though he has to drag the other finalist out to the proposal spot and break her heart first.

Okay! Now that we're all onboard, I shall proceed with my case study of *The Bachelor* and *The Bachelorette* television seasons, just like they do at Harvard Business School, only without all the assholes.

With the exception of Season 17's Sean Lowe, a highly religious and all-around-good guy who had a sincere desire to find love during his season's filming, most of the Bachelors have been simultaneously flummoxed and delighted by the array of beautiful women to choose among. Even toward the very end of their seasons, the men always seemed to be torn among several women. Left to their own devices, many of the Bachelors would still be dating all 25 women.

The show does its best to hide it, but the Bachelorettes generally key in on one or two men quite early. (I gleaned this from the online message boards, including one spoiler website. Yep, I spend my free time productively.)

The women generally spend most of the season trying to figure out which of their few favorites are the most trustworthy, and also the most desirous of a long-term relationship.

As a case in point, on the very first *Bachelorette*, Trista chose the romantic, poetry-writing Ryan, over the glamorous but clearly less-than-ready-to-settle-down Charlie.

It's important to remember, for the purposes of this case study, that the entire premise of the show is that the Bachelor or the Bachelorette is going to become engaged at the show's last filming. That's what the Bachelors and the Bachelorettes sign up for. This is a group that has sworn to the producers and casting directors that they are ready for love.

So. Out of 19 *The Bachelor* seasons, how many men, would you think, have married the woman they've chosen on the final show?

Here's the answer: one. Exactly one Bachelor, out of nineteen, has married the woman he proposed to at the end of the show. I'm not a statistician, but those are bad odds.

Let me quickly recap all 19 *The Bachelor* seasons:

One of the Bachelors ended up marrying the woman he proposed to at the end of the show. (That would be Sean. Jason ended up marrying his second choice after dumping the woman he'd proposed to on the show's final episode on an after-the-season live special. That poor woman—Melissa Rycroft—went on to *Dancing with the Stars* fame, so we don't have to worry about her.)

Seven of the Bachelors couldn't bring themselves to propose, despite it being the entire premise of the show (Alex, Bob, Jesse, Charlie, Travis, Prince Lorenzo, Juan Pablo). Instead, they chose one woman at the end of the show to continue dating, tepidly declaring their love. (Except Juan Pablo, who famously refused to tell Nikki he loved her, which argument continued on *Couples Therapy* on VH1. Which I also watched.)

One of the seven Bachelors who couldn't bring himself to propose, Bob Guiney, who was rumored to have won the prize for having slept with the most contestants during the show's taping, dropped his final choice, the elegant Estella, for an actress on *All My Children* only weeks after the show's final episode aired.

Nine of the Bachelors proposed and then proceeded to break up with their fiancées within a couple months of the show, often within weeks (Aaron, Andrew F., Andrew B., Matt, Jake, Jason, Brad, Ben, Chris). Jake was most probably dumped by Vienna, and Brad may have been dumped by Emily after she watched the season unfold on TV and got a chance to see how very interested he was in other women right up until the end of the show's filming, but the important point here is that all these nine *Bachelor* relationships that started with proposals did not last .

Two of the Bachelors proposed and the relationships lasted for five years before a break-up, with no marriage (Byron, Charlie).

One of the Bachelors chose no one. (Brad, in his first season. They let him try again, after therapy.)

Amusingly, two of the above Bachelors proposed to women so thoroughly disliked by the other women that they spent much of the show warning the Bachelor about her. Predictably, both relationships came to a screeching halt after the show ended and before any marriage vows were exchanged.

After 19 seasons of *The Bachelor*, the conclusions are inescapable. Men, given the choice of 25 beautiful women:

1. Became confused.
2. Wanted to sample as many of the goods as possible (I'm talking to you, Bob Guiney).

3. Have trouble maintaining their commitment much past the show's final airing.

So, you might ask, how did the Bachelorettes do in the choosing department? Well, let's see. Since 2003, there have been 11 seasons of *The Bachelorette*.

Three Bachelorettes are currently married to the man they chose on the show (Trista, Ashley, Desiree). Trista married Ryan, and Ashley married J.P., after their shows ended. Both couples are now parents and blissfully happy, at least according to *US Weekly*. Desiree married the sweet mortgage consultant Chris in early 2015.

Three Bachelorette seasons ended in relationships that lasted for over a year (Meredith, Jillian, Ali). Meredith then got dumped because her fiancée couldn't see himself with a wife and three children or maybe it was a wife and two children, but whatever the problem was, he couldn't commit. The poor woman was later featured on the cover of *People Magazine* for having conquered the drinking problem she developed after being on the show.

One Bachelorette had an engagement that lasted 7 months (DeAnna).

One Bachelorette, Kaitlyn, is currently engaged to her intense personal trainer, Shawn, whom she apparently bonded with early in the process.

Of the remaining **three** Bachelorettes, no one knows why Emily and Jef broke up but Jef got his fledgling clean water business name out there so that worked out well for him, if not so well for Emily, who later married someone who went to her church. Jen, faced with perhaps the worst group of male choices ever, chose no one. Andi and her hunky, highly enthused baseball player Josh split up right after appearing at the next *The Bachelor* premiere party, much to my surprise, and Chris Harrison's.

So, statistically speaking, if you define a "successful relationship" as one in which the couple either 1) got engaged on the show and then got married, or 2) os currently engaged, or 3) had a relationship that lasted over one year, here are the stats:

> *Out of 19 seasons, The Bachelor ended up with a* **16 percent** *success rate, and marriage percent rate of 6 percent.*
>
> *Out of 11 seasons, The Bachelorette ended up with a* **73 percent** *success rate, with a marriage rate of 33 percent.*

So. When given a platter of gorgeous choices, which sex can't choose or chooses wrong or doesn't want to commit or wants to see what else is out there? Which sex cannot handle all the choices?

Yep, it's the men. Just as it is on *The Bachelor* and *The Bachelorette*, so it is in the online dating world. When faced with an array of attractive mate choices, women are able to both choose and commit.

Men with choices are a hot mess.

6

Help! I'm in a Shopping Cart and I Can't Get Out

For some of us, having one's photo displayed on an online dating website feels uncomfortably like being a product on an e-commerce site. It's like you're a cable cashmere sweater or a pair of no-underwear yoga pants, waiting hopefully for the right man to choose your style and color-combination.

Unsurprisingly, participants in an online dating study in California described the large dating website as a "supermarket" and a "catalog." Some of them even referred to their profile as their "resume," which is taking online dating a bit too seriously, in my humble opinion.

The study's co-authors found that the dating site participants looked for reasons "to filter people out, rather than in," and that online daters slipped easily into viewing one another as commodities in a marketplace.

One male study participant casually admitted to a "find my flaw mentality," which mindset may be why so many online dates seem to have a strange, interview-like feel. I communicated once with a very attractive, very successful man who made me go through two lengthy, 45-minute, job-interview-like phone calls before our first date. He continued to grill me over dinner, and it all ended with—you guessed it—no second date for me.

One of my first online dates was with a financial executive who admitted that he'd had something like eighty online dates in the last year, but that he rarely asked a woman on a second date. He remarked casually that the large dating site we'd met on was "like a candy store." Like, it was his candy store of love. I ordered another glass of Chardonnay, trying to decide if I was an M&M, or a Snickers bar, or probably something more tart, like a Green Apple Skittle.

Candy Store Man still writes me sometimes, two and a half years after our one and only drink date, to tell me about a wine tasting or cultural event. I checked recently and he was still active on the dating website. In fact, he'd been active within the hour.

Bless his heart, as we say in the South, but I think he got lost in the swirling vortex of choice, waiting for Godot, or maybe Jessica Chastain.

Or maybe he was someone the academic researchers who've delved into the mystery of choice call a maximizer.

Maximizers vs. Satisficers

Do you know someone who always has to have the TV remote nearby, ready to switch to another channel? Or has to exhaustively search every kind of LCD television or espresso machine before deciding which one to buy? This person is called a *maximizer*. I have a friend who did extensive research on a variety of dog breeds before she ordered her Havanese puppy from an expensive breeder online. And she still wonders if she should have chosen a Cavalier King Charles Spaniel instead.

On the other hand, there's the person who stops into the dog pound and picks the dog that wags its tail at her. What kind of breed was it? Oh, who cares – the puppy had such cute eyes! And that person, who wanders into the pound for a dog and never looks back, is called a *satisficer*. Yep, satisficer is word. You can even play it in Scrabble, if you want.

Psychologist Barry Schwartz formulated a quiz to determine if you're a maximizer or a satisficer. You score it by noting how strongly you agree or disagree with statements like the following:

- I'm a big fan of lists that attempt to rank things (the best movies, the best singers, the best athletes, the best novels, etc.)
- I never settle for second best.
- I treat relationships like clothing: I expect to try a lot on before finding a perfect fit.

I would imagine Candy Store Man is working on his list of "best jazz musicians of all-time" as we speak. In an interesting twist, researchers have found that maximizers often end up making worse choices for themselves, even after all their searching. In a recent Taiwanese study, researchers found that online dating maximizers ended up choosing women further from their originally stated preferences.

And there's more. Once maximizers finally choose, studies have found they feel more regret about their decisions (like my friend and her Havanese puppy). Maximizers are also less satisfied with life *and* more likely to suffer from depression.

If you know a maximizer who discarded you for an upgraded brand or just moved on right past you, rest easy that he will probably lead a life filled with regrets, both large and small.

I've got to say; we satisficers always knew our way of choosing was better. And we're used to the disdain of the maximizers when we make a quick and easy choice. I once bought a car that I had never even heard of before that very day. I went to a dealership to drive a Prius and couldn't see out the back window, drove a Scion on the same lot, loved the rocking sound system, bought the car and went home. I still remember a friend asking me if I'd given it enough thought. Damn straight I gave it enough thought! I could see clearly out the back window and I liked the sound system. It didn't have to be any more complicated than that.

7

So Much Choice, So Easy to Move On

"Men are only as faithful as their options."
–Chris Rock

Women Online Dating Significantly Outnumber the Men

I was continually astonished that the men online seemed to be so much pickier than they were offline. If I didn't answer an email quickly enough, I was dropped. If I didn't answer whatever intrusive question I was posed at dinner or over drinks, I was dropped. I remember thinking, "Do only supermodels live in my Florida beachside community? How could the men online possibly be so ridiculously picky, and so very, very confident?"

And then I found out why. (Note the bolds, and the italics.) I discovered a website where advertisers sign up to place ads on OkCupid, Match, OurTime, Chemistry, and BlackPeople-

Meet. (All of these websites are owned by the same corporation.)

The website reveals how many subscribers on each of these sites are male versus female. (Because the advertisers can choose to target their ads just to the male or female subscribers.)

And here, my dear readers, is our problem, in a nutshell. ***There are massively more women than men on the dating websites.*** (Note the bolds, and the italics.) For all the complaining that men do about how difficult it is for men to online date, here are the real figures I found as to how many men versus women are on the major dating websites (at the time of writing this book):

PERCENTAGES OF MEN VERSUS WOMEN ON THE MAJOR DATING WEBSITES

OkCupid:

- 29 % Male
- 71 % Female

Match:

- Male: 39%
- Female: 61%

OurTime:

- Male: 37%
- Female: 63%

Chemistry:

- Male: 34%
- Female: 66%

BlackPeopleMeet:

- Male: 36%
- Female: 64%

In a nutshell, we women are fucked from the start. There are too few men on the dating websites, and too many of us. I admit to feeling both astonishment and some degree of relief when I saw the real figures. I'd always assumed that there were approximately equal numbers of men and women on the dating websites. It made my experiences with the oddly choosy men seem more understandable.

An older *New York Times* article tagged the percentage of women on eHarmony at 68.6 percent, which makes sense given that men on the website must wait to be matched, which is more appealing to women. eHarmony is also known as the most marriage-minded of the websites, an additional turn-off to some men.

And the question then becomes: what can women expect when they online date, given the lopsided percentages? According to my own figures, some of the men who online date are players, some are creeps, and some want women significantly younger than themselves. How, then, could women expect to have satisfactory experiences dating online?

The answer, of course, is that we usually don't. I will say this for OkCupid: at least it's free. When subscribing to Match, Chemistry, OurTime, BlackPeopleMeet, or eHarmony, women pay for the privilege of fighting for a small group of entitled men.

Do you know what the definition of a 29 percent male to a 71 percent female ratio is? I do. It's called *a losing battle*. (Note the bolds, and the italics.)

How Can We Measure Up? We Can't

Once you know that the odds are stacked against you, much of the male behavior online starts to make more sense. My girlfriends and I had discovered, much to our dismay, that our online dates continued to be demanding once we'd started a relationship. Like it had become their birthright.

I became involved with a business consultant whom I'd met online who I initially was very enthused about. We had the same sense of humor and he seemed delighted to have a real connection with me. It became clear to me within a short period of time, however, that he felt I was lucky he'd stopped his game of musical chairs for me. I soon felt like I was on super-secret probation, just like John Belushi's frat in *Animal House*.

I cooked various meals for him, always following his casually dropped suggestions. (Did I like tomato mozzarella salads? He did! And could I use the fresh basil from his garden!)

One night, after I made a delicious (and easy!) sautéed grouper with baby bok choy and a soy-ginger vinaigrette from my mom's *Le Bernardin Cookbook*, we watched some motocross races that he had taped. After a few races, he questioned me—looking intently interested—as to whether I was enjoying watching the races, because he *loved* motocross racing. I politely replied that I was. (I'll watch anything on TV, I mean, I watched Flavor Flav try to find a wife).

Looking satisfied with my answer, he then asked me if I wanted to go fishing with him the next morning. Startled, I agreed, and he promptly fired up his computer and had me buy my own fishing license. (I'm hoping it doesn't automatically renew.)

I apparently passed the fishing test with flying colors and the next week he asked me if I liked to roller blade. I replied that I used to have roller blades, but that I no longer had them, hoping that would be the end of that subject. (Do people still roller blade? I digress.)

Instead, we jumped into his car and headed to a sporting goods store so that I could buy myself a new pair of roller blades, though as luck would have it, they didn't have a pair he approved of in my size. (Do people still roller blade? I digress.)

A few days later, he took me to a biking shop to pick up an accessory for his expensive road bike. He had me test drive a few bikes and he was clearly irked when I declined to buy a new $900 bike to accompany him on his 20-mile rides. (I told him that I already had a bike, albeit an older one).

My erstwhile Lance Armstrong sent me a curt break-up email the next day in which he said we "didn't have enough in common," and directed me to drive the forty minutes to his house to return a pair of earphones, which were to be left on his front porch. To no one's surprise in this universe—and in parallel universes, too—he was back online that very night. (Sometimes I wished I could add captions to my dates' profile photos, like "Must like biking in 90 degree heat, and endless episodes of *Monty Python*.")

I could write this a thousand different times or in a thousand different ways, but I'll just write it once and then we can stare sadly at it for a moment: Given the endless alternatives, it's simply too easy for a man to move on.

For some men, the endless alternatives are the essential appeal of online dating. Former *Wall Street Journal* reporter Dan Slater, whose parents met on some sort of early Harvard matching experiment, recently wrote a wrote a well-publicized book about the online dating industry entitled *Love in the Time of Algorithms: What Technology Does to Meeting and Mating.*

In his book, Slater describes an online dater in Portland, Oregon named Jacob who was cleaning up on the online dating websites:

> "It was fairly incredible ... I'm an average-looking guy. I wasn't used to picking and choosing that way. All of a sudden I was going out with one or two very pretty, ambitious women a week. At first I just thought it was some kind of weird lucky streak."

At one point lucky Jacob found himself inadvertently sleeping with three women at the same time, while also seeing a few other women. He started feeling kind of badly about it when one of the women told him how much she valued finding an honest man.

Jacob opined that he probably would have married another woman he met online, if he'd only met her offline, before the advent of online dating.

Slater attempts to place online dating in a historical perspective, asserting that in the not so distant past, love and commitment stemmed from a scarcity of people, and that people got married partially because of a lack of options. He opines that the new online world has made dating more sexually casual and less monogamous, and that's just the way things are going to be from now on and no one can do anything about it.

He quotes Greg Blatt, the then CEO of Match's parent company, who is a bachelor in his forties, "You could say online dating is simply changing people's ideas about whether commitment itself is a life value." (Sometimes, I think women are from Venus and men are from, well, it rhymes with well.)

And then Slater quotes Neil Beiderman, the then CEO of Ashley Madison, who makes his own case against monogamy, "I often wonder whether matching you up with great people is getting so efficient, and the process so enjoyable, that marriage will become obsolete." (Yep, men are from Hell.)

Slater spends five pages glowingly describing Beiderman's business model and Ashley Madison's 13 million members worldwide before writing approvingly:

"His efforts don't seem as outlandish when you think of the ways our views on relationships—from premarital sex, to divorce, to gay marriage—have progressed over the years."

(As we now know, reports from the recent Ashley Madison database dump indicate that the vast majority of the clientele was made up of men, and further, many of the female profiles were inactive and possibly fake.)

To Slater, the new "no monogamy" that men are pushing upon women on dating websites could be viewed as a normal technological change. Like, say, electric heat or 3-D glasses at the movies.

Other commentators of online dating have also pointed out that more choice equals less commitment. But rather than celebrating this new world of lowered commitment, they're clearly concerned.

French sociologist Jean-Claude Kaufmann wrote an entire book, *Love Online*, about the brand new world of online dating. He warned, "The internet is changing the game of the rules of love." And in that new world, he writes, "No one has a compass."

Describing the merry-go-round of lovers online, he laments that the "all-pervasive cynicism and utilitarianism eventually sicken anyone who has any sense of human decency."

Another Frenchman, philosopher Alain Badiou, clearly agrees. In his recent book, *In Praise of Love,* he criticizes the ads for Meetic, France's largest online dating site.

Badiou thinks the Meetic ads give the impression that love will be easy. He writes, "We could say that love is a tenacious adventure … To give up at the first hurdle, the first serious disagreement, the first quarrel, is only to distort love."

Badiou passionately declares at one point, "The women I have loved I have loved for always."

I'm not a crier, but that kind of brought a little tear to my eye, though I am of the strongly held opinion that the word "love" should not be mentioned in a book about online dating.

If Alain Badiou were on OkCupid they'd have to kick him off so that he wouldn't make all the other men look so bad. I would like to dedicate an entire chapter to Alain Badiou and his ideas of grand passion, but this book is about the horror hell-world of online dating, so I shall move on.

Some People, Um, Move On A Lot

In the middle of what Florida calls winter, in a bit of a dating drought, I got an email from a man who sounded really nice. His initial email to me was almost chivalrous in its wording.

We agreed to meet at a downtown Sarasota bistro and two nights later I was sipping a glass of red wine and my handsome, charming date was drinking a Scotch. At first, the date seemed to be going swimmingly. He was a great conversationalist, and appeared to be quite taken with me. He was telling me how much he wanted to get off the dating site we'd met on, as if it were a tedious process for him, like it is for most people.

I was sort of warming to him until he started to talk about a well-known friend of his. He began regaling me with stories about how his famous friend could get "laid" all day long, if he wanted. He described it admiringly, as if that were a legitimate aspirational goal, like curing melanoma.

I took another sip of my glass of wine and asked him how many women he'd slept with. Yep, I went there. I softened it up a little, like I think I asked him if he'd had the same sort of luck, like how many women had he slept with?

He looked over at me assessingly, and I smiled sweetly back at him. In the heavily Scandinavian state where I grew up, the way we act has nothing at all to do with what we're thinking inside. It's confusing, but you learn to read the signals when you grow up there. He didn't read mine.

He half-smiled as he answered, looking proud. "I've been online dating for over five years and I've probably slept with…" He paused for a moment to think. "… Three hundred women." He'd borrowed my glasses earlier to read the menu and I inched my hand across the table to retrieve them, wondering if I should Purell them later. He added, "I've never worn condoms and I've never had an STD." Sweet-Mary-Mother-of-God. I was going to have to throw my glasses away.

The waitress came over and I ordered a martini, which my smiling date took as a sign of interest, though I had no intention of being number 301. I'd taken a taxi to the bistro and I was free—free!—to drink as much as I wanted, and drinking was what I planned to do.

When I got home that night, a bit tipsy but no worse for the wear, I tumbled into bed, thankful to be alone. It could be the new online dating serenity prayer:

"Thank you, Lord, that I am alone and not with an asshole tonight."

Marriages and Relationships that Start Online End Earlier

Recent research has revealed—cue the drum rolls—that the pesky problem of "too many alternatives" keeps popping up in long-term relationships and marriages that began online.

A groundbreaking 2014 study out of Michigan State University turned the online dating world on its side, or at least tilted it a little. An enterprising doctoral candidate named Aditi Paul analyzed the data from 4,000 marriages and long-term relationships and discovered the following astonishing, previously unknown information:

> Relationships and marriages that started online were *more likely* to break up than relationships that started offline. In fact, Paul found that online marriages were *four times* more likely to break up than marriages that started offline.

And the couples who met online were significantly less likely to get married in the first place: only 32 percent of online couples got married, versus 67 percent of the couples who met offline.

That's pretty amazing information, if you think about it. Paul theorized that the reason online relationships and marriages are more likely to break up is because of the "knowledge of alternatives."

So the endless, tantalizing parade of online profiles continues to be a cloud over the relationships and marriages that start online. It's like a heavy gray fog that just won't lift.

So is it the same for men and women, you might ask? Do the sexes feel the same "attention to alternatives" that leads to decreased commitment levels?

What would your guess be?

John Lydon, a McGill professor who specializes in relationship commitment issues, succinctly sums up the evidence:

> "Across studies, men exhibited the responses that traditional commitment theories hypothesize – an increase in the availability of alternatives lead to a decrease in commitment-related behavior."

In other words, men felt less commitment given more alternatives. Lydon found that women "did the reverse," and, in fact, showed an increased "willingness to accommodate and tolerate a romantic partner's transgressions."

So, given more attractive alternatives, men stray more, and women tolerate more. Again, quelle surprise.

In the online dating world, my girlfriends and I often met men who were currently dating other women. I'm not talking about dinner and coffee dates. I'm talking about we often met men who were clearly in sexual relationships with other women. It's just the new normal of online dating. And you start to think, well, he hasn't known me that long. Surely I can't expect him not to be seeing two or three other women, or even going with them on weekend trips or cruises, or indeed, trips to Europe.

The problem is, how can that be a good start to a healthy relationship? When you read the lovely back stories in the *New York Times* wedding section, is that how the couples met and married? With the man frantically checking out every woman he could while his future fiancée patiently waited for him to fall for her? No, of course not. But in the bizarro world of online dating, you become numb to normality.

At one point in my online dating journey, I dated a banker who was really, really smart. I think he had the highest IQ of all the men I met online, and that was a potent aphrodisiac for me.

He was also an expert cook, which made me like him even more. Food is my family's hobby. If we had a family crest (which we wouldn't) it would be two crossed lollipop lamb chops, perfectly herbed. Other families bond with camping or cruising or tailgating at football games, but for fun, my family cooks and eats.

On one of my first dates with my new beau, we went to a Chinese market and picked out beef stomach for him to cook up, Creole style. (It's kind of chewy, like calamari, but surprisingly good.)

Shortly thereafter, we drove to a hunting cabin he owned a few hours away. On the freeway trip there, I discovered that he was in a two-year relationship with someone else. When I became, well, somewhat upset, he accused me of being a "buzz-killer" to his weekend.

I settled myself down, since my only other choice was to

abandon him at a rest stop and hope to meet someone better, which I thought was unlikely. That night, when I tentatively brought up the girlfriend issue again, he explained that he would certainly break up with her if he got to know me better and started liking me more, but it would be unreasonable to expect him to break up with her for me since "he knew her so much better."

I had no real comeback for that, so I just enjoyed my wine and bourbon and the wild boar he cooked up, which later made me puke my guts out by the side of the bed while he desperately attempted to coax me into the bathroom, which made me feel a little better about the weekend. I mean, I may have dated a bit of an ass, but at least I got to throw up on him.

Drinking and Online Dating

You may or may not have noticed, but some of my online dating stories involve some degree of alcohol imbibing. Drinking could be considered as yet another drawback of online dating, or you could place it within the context of the development of human civilization.

I read an interesting article in *National Geographic* that theorized that civilization and organized communities were formed because of people's desire for alcohol. Former hunters and gatherers realized that they had to settle in small communities in one place to grow grain, and what they wanted to make with that grain was beer.

Clearly, we'd still be roaming the plains hoping to spear a Mastodon if early humans didn't enjoy their alcohol. So I've decided not to place copious drinking on the list of shortcomings of online dating. If you don't agree, all I have to say is this: you try online dating for a week without alcohol, and then report back to me.

What it Means When He Won't Take His Profile Down

In yet another intriguing finding, Rowland Miller, author of a study titled *"Inattentive and Contented: Relationship Commitment and Attention to Alternatives,"* found that there is "No better predictor of relationship failure than high attentiveness to alternatives." And as every woman who's online dated knows, one potent sign that a man is displaying "high attentiveness to alternatives" is just how active he remains on a dating website.

It's one of the most vexing annoyances of online dating. You can be dating someone and things seem to be going well and then you discover that Mr. Right is still active online. His profile is still up, and, to make things worse, he's on every night. Hell, he's on every time you check. He may indeed have quit his job so that he can be online every fucking second of his motherfucking day. (Oops! Got a little carried away there.)

When I was online dating, I used my old computer with another sign-in name and email—thanks, Mom!—to anonymously check to see how active my dates were on the dating site.

Every once in a while I'd admit to a man that I'd checked on him. One man whom I dated was online more than I would have expected. When I screwed up the courage to casually ask him about it, he replied that he only got on Match to send nice 'no thanks' notes back to the women who'd contacted him. He then took it a bit too far and actually said that he admired their courage for contacting him. I still remember how amused I was when he said that. I mean, if you're going to be a player, you're going to need more game than that.

Checking to see if someone you're dating is active on a dating website is admittedly a little creepy, but the problem is that it does truly mean something. It turned out that Mr. Concerned About the Women Who Wrote Him was dating so many women that one night after we'd talked on the phone he immediately called again and identified himself as "Mike from Match," a call clearly meant for the next woman on his list.

A man interested in a relationship with you isn't constantly online, checking out the alternatives. An interested man isn't on the dating site the second he gets home from a date. And a man who wants to develop a good relationship with you is all too happy to take his profile down. Alain Badiou would take his profile down. Hell, Alain Badiou would pop open a bottle of champagne and make a celebration of it.

There's a really cool principle called "Occam's Razor." All it means is that the simplest, most logical explanation is usually the correct explanation. If a man remains active online while he's dating you, he's not really interested. If Juan Pablo of *The Bachelor* fame won't tell Nikki he loves her, it's because he doesn't love her. Sometimes we women just make things too complicated.

8

The Accursed Players

"Women might be able to fake orgasms, but men
can fake whole relationships."
–Anonymous

"You already have one asshole, you don't need
another one."
–Greg Behrendt and Liz Tuccillo, *He's Just Not That
Into You: The No-Excuses Truth to Understanding
Guys*

What Women Want

Let me start this chapter with a couple out-and-out asser-
tions about women. Women want *relationships* with the men
they have sex with. They want emotion and kindness and care,
along with the sex. Without that, they don't want sex, or at
least not for long. Women want the cute Scottish policeman
in the movie *Bridesmaids,* not Jon Hamm in the movie, or in
Mad Men, either.

Indeed, women are so uninterested in casual sex that

researchers have theorized that friends with benefits relationships are a compromise relationship between a more invested woman and a less emotionally invested man. A recent study found that 69 percent of women in a friends with benefits relationship were hoping that the relationship would develop into something more, but 60 percent of men wanted the relationship to stay the same.

Anthropologist and sexual behavior researcher John Townsend observed that females in sexual relationships, "[In which] They desired more investment than partners were willing to give produced feelings of distress, degradation, and exploitation…."

Numerous other studies have shown that women feel regret, distress and negative reactions following a hookup. The co-authors of a study of casual sexual encounters at a large Southeastern university warned "women are at substantially more risk than men for feeling upset about the experience."

In an oft-quoted study, male and female researchers stopped opposite sex students at a university and asked if that person wanted to come over to their apartment that night and go to bed with them. Over 75 percent of the male students said yes, and most of the rest explained apologetically that they had a girlfriend, or that they could meet another time, or immediately. Exactly zero percent of the female students agreed to have casual sex with a complete stranger.

Have I made my point that women don't want emotionless sex? Nope, not yet. Not by a long shot.

After doing more Harvard-math-major numbers crunching Christian Rudder of OkCupid discovered that 0.8 percent of their website's straight female members are openly looking for a casual sexual relationship. He opined that it was because women didn't want to seem sexually forward. (Um, no. Don't opine for us.)

I don't mean to beat a dead horse (yes I do), but women are so uninterested in casual sex that Markus Frind, the CEO of POF, ended up deleting POF's "intimate encounters" relationship category in 2013, reporting that only 6,041 women of POF's 3.3 million members had checked "intimate encounters" as a relationship category they would be interested in. (Frind also offered up that most of those 6,041 were probably "horny men pretending to be women.")

But Yet!

But yet! There are men on the online dating websites—all over the online dating websites—who think they have a right to impose their desire for serial short-term relationships upon women who *clearly* don't want that.

What kind of man does this? What kind of man uses and exploits women for his own personal satisfaction with an egocentric lack of empathy for the women whom he exploits?

The *players*, that's who. If I could make the word *players* burst into flames on this page, I would.

And where is the perfect place for a *player* to *play*?

Online. On a dating system designed almost perfectly to facilitate the worst of players' instincts for women as prey.

The Dark Triad

Fascinating research over the past ten years has shown that men who prefer short, exploitative relationships often have a combination of toxic traits called the Dark Triad. It sounds like something from one of those interminable action movies made for $200 million that appeal only to men. And in this case, it *does* usually refer to men. Researchers have found that significantly more men than women have one or a combination of the following personality traits: Machiavellianism, narcissism, and psychopathy.

The social science academic worlds have been abuzz in recent years linking people who are high in the Dark Triad traits to a variety of undesirable behaviors, like internet trolling, being a nightmare boss, and yep—you guessed it—a penchant for short-term, exploitative relationships.

I'm going to start my tour of the Dark Triad with Machiavellianism. This personality trait was named after a 16th-century Italian nobleman named Niccolò Machiavelli, who wrote a book about getting ahead in the political world by whatever means possible, including lying and projecting an incorrect image to fool others. If there had been online dating back then, Niccolò would have been all over it.

The second of the Dark Triad traits is narcissism, which is typified by a sense of personal superiority, along with a craving for admiration and attention from others. If you're dating a narcissist, you exist to please him.

The third and worst of the Dark Triad traits is psychopathy, which is typified by a remorseless personal style. Many, if not most people, who fall into the psychopath category are in the high-functioning range, which means they show psychopathic tendencies but aren't Ted Bundy psycho-killers.

In the relationship world, researchers have linked these three undesirable personalities to a heartless, game-playing dating style, and to a preference for short-term, exploitative relationships. In other words, these are the bastards to watch out for.

Narcissists have been shown to prefer friends with benefits relationships and casual hookups, which allow them to continue seeking the attention of others without getting too involved. Machiavellians get the casual sex they want by ruthlessly lying about their involvement and intentions in a relationship. And psychopaths prefer booty calls and one-night stands, which is not surprising, as these relationships suit their emotionally shallow natures.

Sadly, all three personality types don't care if they hurt you, because at the core of all three is a lack of empathy for others.

Unfortunately for us, online dating has given members of the Dark Triad a free reign formerly unbeknownst in the history of the world. With no shared community to warn us about the players—and without any consequences to their actions—the online dating sites have become the players' personal playgrounds of love.

Two intrepid psychologists, Peter Jonason and George Webster, developed a quick test to check for Dark Triad tendencies.

The Dark Triad Test

Members of the Dark Triad tend to agree with the following statements:

1. I tend to manipulate others to get my way.
2. I have used deceit or lied to get my way.
3. I have use flattery to get my way.
4. I tend to exploit others towards my own end.
5. I tend to lack remorse.
6. I tend to be unconcerned with the morality of my actions.
7. I tend to be callus or insensitive.
8. I tend to be cynical.
9. I tend to want others to admire me.
10. I tend to want others to pay attention to me.
11. I tend to seek prestige or status.
12. I tend to expect special favors from others.

Questions 1-4 relate to Machiavellianism, questions 5-8 to psychopathy, and questions 9-12 to narcissism.

Each question is supposed to be scored on a seven-point scale but I think it's easy enough to score: if you 'tend" to agree with many of the above statements, you're officially a shithead.

I'm going to delve more deeply into each of the Dark Triad personality types so that you can avoid them as much as possible, before you have the kind of bad experience with one that perhaps only electroshock therapy will remove from your brain, or, someday, Alzheimer's.

Narcissists

People *like* narcissists, at least until they get to know them better. Narcissists' charm allows them to easily begin new relationships, and their egocentrism allows them to easily move on.

One study concluded that narcissists "view their sexual partners as objects that satisfy their needs for pleasure, status, and power." The co-authors found that narcissists linked words like "domination," "influence," "manipulation," and "daring" to sex, rather than "loyalty," "trust," and "closeness," like us normal, non-narcissistic folk.

Not surprisingly, narcissists often cheat in their relationships, probably to feed their egos and their endless desire for admiration. Narcissists are in relationships for what they can get out of them—including status, sex, and attention—so it's not surprising that researchers have also learned that caring and emotional intimacy are not what narcissists are looking for in their relationships.

All of which probably explains social psychologist Joshua Foster's observation that the ex-partners of narcissists "report being particularly unsettled by their relationships."

How to Spot a Narcissist in the Wild

Well! Now that we know we should stay away from narcissists, how can we spot 'em in the wild? Here's some help:

Clues you might be dating a narcissist

- He flirts with other women, waitresses, and your friends.
- He's cheated on past girlfriends or spouses.
- He hangs with wingmen friends.
- He doesn't know how many siblings you have. Or where you went to college.
- He uses sexual words, especially "fuck," in normal conversation.
- He likes friends with benefits relationships.
- He puts others down.
- He's obsessed with how his hair looks. And his abs.
- He wants the best of everything: shoes, cars, clothes, and women.
- He loves to talk about himself.
- He's always on the look-out to trade up to a higher prestige girlfriend.
- He may try to talk you into sexual acts you might be uncomfortable with.
- When he feels insulted, he verbally attacks.
- He thinks some of the normal rules of life don't apply to him.
- You exist to please him.
- You exist to please him.

Here's another clue: a narcissist views how you look as a reflection upon him. I once dated a man who informed me while out to lunch one day that my sandals looked "slovenly." He seemed surprised that I was somewhat dismayed by his comment. I got on my iPhone and did a search for exactly what "slovenly" meant, since he seemed unwilling to discuss it any further.

My quick search revealed that the synonyms for "slovenly" included "slatternly" and "slutty," though in my date's defense, Wikipedia only defined it as "unwashed, dirty and disorderly."

Did I mention that my sandals were very cute flats from an expensive shoe store? And, needless to say, clean?

We got into sort of an argument in which he continued to defend his right to let me know what shoes he did like, which were Coach.

Since I am sometimes an idiot I continued to date him and then it turned out that he was dating a bunch of other people, too, like we were his harem of Coach-shoed women.

If I'd known what I know now, I could have saved myself some heartache. It would have occurred to me: "Hmmm… He wants me to wear the Coach shoes he likes and is willing to insult me to do it, so perhaps I'm dating a narcissist."

Then I could have asked him telling questions like, "Do you tend to seek prestige or status?" from the Dark Triad test above, and extricated myself from the relationship earlier, like right after lunch.

In Greek mythology, Narcissus fell in love with his own reflection in a pool of water and fell in and died, which is both sad and funny. And that's all I have to say about that.

Onward to Machiavellian Asses.

Machiavellians

Machiavellians are the cold-hearted bastards of the dating world. To them, 'the ends justify the means.' Not surprisingly, studies have linked Machiavellianism to success selling cars, stocks, and real estate.

Machiavellians are the most cynical and immoral of the Dark Triad and they've been found to be particularly manipulative when it comes to romance. They're "love-feigners," willing to lie about their intentions and their interest in a relationship to get what they want. Another coercive method they've been found to use with their lucky dates is "inducing intoxication for sex."

If a sneaky Machiavellian you meet online is involved with another woman, you'd only be able to drag that information out of his cold, dead, crafty hands.

Interestingly, the research has shown that Machiavellians aren't smarter than everyone else; it's just that they're more willing to deceive to achieve their goals.

How to Spot a Machiavellian in the Wild

Machiavellians operate more under the radar compared to psychopaths or narcissists. They're not wild thrill-seekers or glib charmers; instead, these are men willing to do whatever it takes to manipulate you to get exactly what they want out of a relationship. They're more likely to be in a long-term relationship than narcissists or psychopaths, but they're equally prone to cheating.

Clues you might be dating a Machiavellian

- He mentions an interest in a long-term relationship, or even marriage, early on to suck you in.
- He's not in a helping profession, nor could you imagine him in one.
- He may value his career above his relationships.
- He's told you more than a few half-truths, or omitted important details in stories.
- He uses flattery to get what he wants.
- He's likely to cheat on his taxes, a term paper, or a lover.
- He may lie about his income or assets.
- He views the world and people in a negative light.
- He has a cynical view of other people's motivations.
- He values power and money.
- He's not interested in volunteer work unless it benefits him in some way.

I had the misfortune of dating a wily Machiavellian while on my online dating journey. I was contacted by a man from a city up North whose profile deceptively indicated that he currently lived about ten minutes from my apartment. When I answered his first email, he casually explained that he was in town for a week, but that he was in the process of moving down here and had been coming down to the same beachside condo for twenty years. (Which naturally made me assume he owned a vacation home in my beachside city.)

If I had known that he was visiting a friend's condo and that he had no plans to move down here—whatsoever, ever—I never would have become involved with him. And Machiavellian that he was, he knew that.

The women in Sarasota who online date are practically besieged by men who come down here for a vacation week or two and want to "get together for dinner or a drink." I'm always been puzzled as to why men think we would be interested in getting together with someone who's just dropped by our city for a visit. Do they think we're tour guides? Or their personal Match.com escort service, but in a new city? (Most likely answer.)

Men's minds puzzle, as always.

Psychopaths

High-functioning psychopaths can utilize their emotionless, aggressive, risk-taking behavior to become very successful. In a research finding that will surprise no one, a study found that psychopaths are found at higher frequencies at financial service institutions.

In the relationship world, psychopaths are thrill-seekers who want to bed as many women as possible, in as many unusual places as possible. Did anybody you dated ever try to drag you into an airplane's filthy restroom for a quickie? Or worse, a bar bathroom? Yep, now you know it's not only unhygienic, it's a possible sign of a thrill-seeking psychopath. (Try using that as an excuse next time.)

Psychopaths love casual sex, and lots of it. In fact, a recent study actually linked a high number of sexual partners, and the enjoyment of casual sex with no feelings of attachment, to *being* a psychopath. (And significantly more men than women are psychopaths. Hmmm… I think I'm seeing a pattern here.)

Psychopaths will get try to get their fill of casual sex any way they can. In a study out of the University of South Carolina, male college students who scored high on the psychopathy scale used flattery, coercion and alcohol to get women to have sex with them, at double the rate of non-psychopathic men. (Only double? Good God.)

And do psychopaths feel badly about the shit they do? Hell to the no. Another major signal that you're dating a psychopath is his complete lack of remorse for anything he does to you, or to anyone else, for that matter.

How to Spot a Psychopath in the Wild

It's odd to think that you might have crossed paths with a psychopath, albeit a high-functioning one. As I've mentioned, booty calls are something to watch out for, which should be answered with a firm message like, "Here's who you can fuck at eleven-fifteen at night: yourself."

Sometimes it's hard to cut a man off. You might think to yourself, hopefully yet delusionally, "Maybe he was just really busy until just now, at eleven-fifteen at night." But here's the deal: the sooner you cut things off with a man who is causing you grief, the better off you'll be.

Clues you might be dating a psychopath

- He lies to get his way. He lies for no reason at all. He just likes to lie.
- He never apologizes.
- He may get pleasure or amusement from the misfortune of others.
- He's into booty calls and hookups.
- He doesn't cry at funerals, movies, or YouTube videos of returning soldiers reuniting with their dogs.
- He's easily bored.
- You sense it would not be a good idea to make him angry.
- He's charming and glib.
- He's impulsive.
- He's a thrill-seeker.
- He rarely gets nervous.
- He may enjoy violent movies and video games.
- He may have a poor relationships with his parents or his children.
- He may like to gamble, ski off-trail, or ride his motorcycle without a helmet.
- He's chronically unfaithful to his sexual partners.

It's illuminating to place men into the high-functioning but psychopathic category. I had a girlfriend who went out with a man a couple times whom she really liked. After they slept together, he immediately stopped taking her out and instead started texting her late at night, asking to come over. I told her about my research into psychopaths and her face lit up. It was relaxing for her to view her recent date's assholeness in the clean, clear light of objective science. It was a sign of his own emotional limitations that he wanted a solely sexual relationship. And he needed to stay as far away from my sweet friend as possible.

Can You Figure Out Early On if a Man is a Player?

Despite our best efforts, it can be tough to pick out a player in the early stages of a relationship. And that makes sense: you are, after all, dealing with a specialist in his field.

When you initially meet a man for coffee, you could try asking your startled date one of the questions in the 12-point Dark Triad test. Most men, however, will not appreciate being polled about whether they "tend to exploit others toward their own end." Your coffee date will likely instead view you as both suspicious, and damaged.

You are, of course, neither suspicious nor damaged, but I've found that men can be surprisingly judgmental if you admit to past bad relationships with players. Instead of being sympathetic, they tend to see you as an injured bird, easy prey for further damage infliction.

Without a shared community of knowledge about a man, which could be gleaned from common acquaintances or work or church or synagogue or Buddhist temple or yoga class, we're left to figure out if a man is a player all on our own.

One of the unfortunate consequences of running into too many players is that it toughens your view of the world. When I watch the news now and some revered public figure is in a sex scandal I think, "Well, yeah, that's just how men are. How could you be surprised?"

In the murky, dark waters of the online dating world, the only way to proceed is with caution. Or perhaps, to redouble your efforts to meet a man offline. Helping out with the local film festival or handing out water bottles at a charity walk leaves you with no emotional scars, unlike dating yet another online player.

If you've had the misfortune to meet and date a player during your online dating stint, be kind to yourself. You might think: How could I have been so stupid? Why didn't I see the red flags?

It's important to forgive yourself for having opened your heart—and perhaps other parts of yourself—to a man who was incapable of real, caring love.

Always remember…

Players are the ones who are damaged, not you.

9

The Ebola Epidemic of Bad Emails and Texts

There is a general impression among male online daters that we women have it easier online. They assume we get tons of delightful messages from charming, likeable men, from whom we pick and choose at our leisure.

Nothing could be further from the truth. Men are as confused about this as they about how much more we pay for our dry cleaning, and our haircuts, too.

When I was on a first date, I would sometimes inquire about how online dating was going for the man sitting across from me. Like, did he have any funny stories? (I never heard one. And they say men are funnier than women.) But my date would invariably recount a sad tale of having met a woman who had lied about her weight or age. And then he would sit back in his chair, looking traumatized.

The indignant man across the table from me should have considered himself blessed, as they say in the South, if a misleading photo or two was the worst thing that ever happened to him while online dating.

It's hard to convince a man how different it is to be a woman online. When I would offer up that I'd received some weird emails, or gone on even weirder dates, they'd scoff. How bad could it have been? And was I somehow bringing it upon myself? (Um, no.)

A reporter named Logan Hill wrote an entertaining article for *New York Magazine*'s fashion website The Cut: "*Meet the 4 Most Desired People in New York (According to OKCupid).*" He'd contacted OkCupid headquarters to try to figure out who were the most popular people in New York City on the dating website and what life was like for them.

The most popular straight guy seemed to be having a gloriously fun time online dating, and didn't know when it would end, if ever.

The most popular straight woman in New York City, a 23-year-old make-up artist, admitted she'd made the mistake of checking—along with an interest in long and short-term relationships—an interest in "casual sex." She got so tired of the dick pics and gross emails she received that she ended up deleting her profile and starting up again with a whole new name. Which didn't seem to be going much better for her.

Sounding bemused, she reported that she still receives email like "I'd so eat you out from behind! :)" on a regular basis, and has only been on about twenty dates in her two years on the dating website. (Who would put a happy face emoticon after "I'd so eat you out from behind"? That's the real story here.)

A Man Gets a Taste of What's It's Like

Apparently, we women can tell men how horrible the

online dating experience is for women all we want, but they don't believe it until they experience it for themselves.

A man posted on a Reddit message board about his unsettling experience as a female on OkCupid. As he recounts it, his grand experiment started when he shared his opinion with a girlfriend that women have it much easier online than men.

She offered to let him use her photo to make a fake OkCupid profile. He set up a profile and only lasted two hours before the inevitable defeat. He wrote of his experience:

> "Guys would become hostile when I told them I wasn't interested in NSA [No Strings Attached] sex, or guys that had started normal and nice quickly turned the conversation into something explicitly sexual in nature. Seemingly nice dudes in quite esteemed careers asking to hook up in 24 hours and sending them naked pics of myself despite multiple times telling them that I didn't want to…I ended up deleting my profile at the end of 2 hours and kind of went about the rest of my night with a very bad taste in my mouth."

His message board confessional was followed by 1,113 basically unsurprised comments from females, most of which were similar to these two:

> "Yeah, if you message a guy back to tell him no, the chances of you getting a 'well you're just a stupid ugly bitch and I was going to slum it with you but whatever whore' message increase exponentially."

"Just another gal saying, yup, that was basically my experience on OKC, too–and 10x worse on POF (couldn't delete that profile fast enough, but there is a 24 wait period to do so)."

I am of the opinion that the magicians who designed the complex mathematical algorithmic formulas at the online dating sites shouldn't have too much trouble figuring out how to better police their members.

Here's my personal message to those cute, geeky math majors who started OkCupid: You can't think of a way to make the experience a little less unsettling for women? Really? Maybe you should try a little harder. *Hah*-vard expects no less from you.

Markus Frind, POF's founder, finally got disgusted with what he had wrought and sent out an email in 2013 to POF's members outlining some new rules, among them that no sexual references could be made in a first email, and that men could no longer attach photos with messages. (Women still can, because they attach photos of their Christmas celebrations, and men attach photos of their dicks.)

I'm not sure what this has done to POF's subscription numbers or ad revenues, but I give Frind props for trying to make the online dating experience slightly less distressing for women.

The Dick Pic Problem

Everyone's got a dick pic story or two, or five, and here's mine.

I had been corresponding with an interesting man who was quite proud of his Mayflower family roots. We'd exchanged a few jokey emails about our very different backgrounds, and as I was driving to the grocery store one morning he sent me a text with a photo of him in a towel. I remember looking at the text photo while at a stoplight and feeling a bit startled, since our last text had been about a book we'd both read, but I sent back something polite, like, "That's a nice pic."

I heard another text ping but I didn't check my phone again until I was in the grocery store. I was in the produce department in front of the avocados next to a nice elderly couple who were squeezing the avocados a little too hard. I opened my latest message to see a photo of my Match correspondent's very erect penis. I mean, his hand was in the photo, too, but you get the idea. Since I'd never met him I was, um, astonished, but no more so than the elderly woman squeezing the avocados next to me, who happened to pick that moment to glance over. I was so embarrassed I abandoned the entire produce department and grabbed a ham and Swiss cheese Lunchable instead.

The next morning, I met a girlfriend for coffee and she looked unsurprised when I spilled my newest story to her. As she buttered her croissant, looking bored, she said that was par for the course with men nowadays. I kept saying, "But I don't even know him!" And she kept saying, "It doesn't matter."

I guess my question is: when did men decide that a woman wants to check out his dick before she meets him? Do men think we're doing a series of calculations, like: okay, you're a Democrat or Republican, check; you're an Aquarius, that's cool; your dick is within acceptable size and girth limits, check, and check. And then we send a text back: "Appreciate you forwarding that key decision-making point, thanks much."

I ended up sending Quick Dick Pic Man a polite email explaining that I really needed to see and appreciate the entire person before that kind of photo became erotic to me. Unsurprisingly, I never heard from him again. (Sometimes I try to help the next woman in line, you know? Though I'm not sure it ever helps.)

Disinhibition

As you might have guessed, the academics have a name for this kind of bad behavior over digital media and it's called "toxic disinhibition."

Without the instant face-to-face feedback of personal interaction, people feel invisible and removed from the consequences of their actions. Researchers have found that people are much more likely to behave in socially acceptable ways online if they have mutual acquaintances, even distant ones. And that makes sense.

I am quite sure that the man who sent me the dick shot would never have sent it to me if we'd had even one acquaintance in common. Do you see how bizarre it starts sounding, if you realize you know the same people? Like, "He did what?! He sent you a photo of his dick?… You'd never even kissed?… Wait, you'd never met?!"

Perhaps I should figure out who my Congressman is and

write to him about the dick pic epidemic. If the federal government can breezily ban trans fat in my beloved Kentucky Fried Chicken Original Recipe, banning a dick pic or two should be no problem.

10

Lies, Scams, and More Lies

"I'm not upset that you lied to me; I'm upset that
from now on I can't believe you."
–Friedrich Nietzsche

I'm not easily shocked. But even I was shocked when I discovered a 2008 press release about Match.com Japan on the website of Match's corporate owner. The press release noted that: "In a recent survey the number one concern of Japanese internet users said they were concerned about the authenticity of other users online." And then a Match senior V.P. was quoted as follows: "We knew we had to address things like identity verification in order to create a truly valuable dating experience for the Japanese consumer."

So here's what Match proposed for its valued users in Japan:

"ID Certification – By allowing users to submit documentation to verify age, gender, marital status, location, income, education, and employment, ID Certification has worked to quell the number one concern regarding online dating: knowing that their potential matches are who they say they are."

So the overlords at Match.com decided, in their infinite wisdom, that the men and women of Japan deserved to feel comfortable that "their potential matches are who they say they are."

But the men and women of the United States of America, apparently, don't deserve to feel that same level of comfort about other users' age, location, income, education, and marital status. Match recently began offering a tepid verification option that confirms whether a user has an email, LinkedIn or Facebook account (but doesn't link you to it; it's a confirmation that you're dealing with a real person), but that is obviously far less than the verification proposed for its Japanese users.

Paul Oyer, an economist and business professor at Stanford who penned his own online dating book—and of course found a wonderful woman in his heartwarming happy ending—wrote an article on *Quartz* about the differences between the more stringent verifications on some Chinese and South Korean online dating sites versus those offered in the United States. He wrote that he hadn't seen much of a call for identity verification in the United States (um, who has he been talking to?), and that the American labor costs to process and verify subscribers' information would be much higher than in China.

Here's how I see it: the Match group's division revenue in 2014 was $836,500,000. (Which includes Match, Chemistry,

OkCupid, Tinder and other dating enterprises in the U.S. and outside it.)

I frankly don't care if identity verification cuts into the Match group's profits. I'm sure Listeria testing cuts into food companies' profits, too, but they do it, in the best interests of their customers.

What say ye, Match? OkCupid? How about you, eHarmony? Just as a start, verifying users' ages is a simple process. What will be the first major dating website to value the integrity of their users' dating experiences over their bottom line?

Somewhat Creative With Their Identity

Just how prevalent is lying online, anyway? One oft-quoted study found that 81 percent of online daters were lying about something, however small. (Including having an older photo.)

Another study found that people online can be "somewhat creative with their identity and presentation of self." Though both men and women can be "somewhat creative," it turns out the men and women lie about very different things.

Let's start with us women. According to studies, we lie more than men about our weight, we use older photos than men, and we touch up our photos more.

And that often bothers the men online, there's no getting around it. But it doesn't scar a man, emotionally, to meet someone for a drink who looks somewhat different than her photos or who is a little heavier than advertised. And in my opinion there's nothing wrong with photoshopping your pics and trying to put up the best picture possible. I would have photoshopped my pictures if I hadn't been too lazy to figure out how to do it. I could have given myself some Kardashian curves to my butt, and maybe some cheekbones, too.

But what about the men? Well, let's just say they can be tricky devils. In one large study of online daters, men were found to lie more than women about income, personal interests, personal attributes, and age. That's a lot of lying.

Numerous studies have found that male online daters also lie significantly more about their current relationship status than women.

I fell into an intense correspondence with a man who turned out to be living with someone else. Here's the sad tale: I was corresponding with a seemingly lovely man who was in the process of buying a second home on a golf course in my resort city. We emailed, we texted, we talked on the phone; and then we made plans to meet when he flew down to close on his new home.

We had been joking about something—to this day I don't remember what—and he sent me a jokey gift of a camouflage vest from an online hunting company.

As I was throwing the gift receipt away, I spotted his street address and decided to Google the shit out of it. After an hour-long search, I finally figured out that he didn't own the house at the address on the receipt—a woman did. I promptly Googled her and found photos of my erstwhile paramour with a very beautiful woman at various events around their city.

I wrote him a polite note including Princess Di's famous statement to Prince Charles when she discovered his relationship with Camilla Parker Bowles: "Three people in a relationship can be a bit crowded."

This earned me a very irate email in which he termed this poor woman a "Friend With Benefits" relationship and then accused me of being "controlling" and "paranoid," which I thought was a little early to be playing the crazy card, considering.

One of my girlfriends suggested that I throw the camo vest away, but I still enjoy wearing it when the weather turns nippy here. It's a damn fine vest, and I figure I got more out of that relationship than I did from most of my relationships that started online.

Back to the studies about lying. Researchers have found that men are more likely to lie online to "achieve short-term goals," which the researchers mean getting a woman into bed. This is a time-honored tactic of men, of course. I'm sure women in caves and sod huts throughout time have sat around complaining about the exact same thing, like, "Yeah, that lying bastard! I actually believed him when he said he wanted to have twenty children with me!"

A recent study from 2010 found that men just are more likely to lie. About anything. They lie to more people, they tell more lies for no reason, and they think they're better liars than women. (I'm not so sure about that.)

Apparently, It's Fun to Make Things Up

I exchanged a couple of emails with a man and we started to make plans to meet. He then proceeded to tell me that he had given his car to his sister, and that he was living in a really dumpy apartment to do research for a book he was writing in which the main character lived in a bad part of town. He told me that he made over $200,000 a year from his business, and then he asked if I could possibly come pick him up, or we could meet somewhere near a bus line.

I politely backed out of our date and he sent me a very irate email in return. It's entirely possible that he is now a best-selling author, but I haven't seen his name yet on the *New York Times* bestseller list. I'll be sure to keep you posted.

On yet another date, I agreed to meet a very handsome lawyer for a drink near where I live. Over our drinks, I asked him where he went to law school and he told me the name of a very fine law school. When I got back home, I looked him up and he had gone to a much lower-ranked law school, which mattered not in the least, since I never heard from him again.

Shortly after that, I went out with a sales rep, and during the course of our one dinner I told him that I really didn't like it when men lied about their age. He agreed vehemently with me and went on quite a rant about honesty and integrity in all matters. I went home, looked up his age on a website I'd found that had that information, and voila! He was lying about his age.

Become Your Own Amateur Detective

About halfway through my online dating journey, I discovered a wonderful website called Lookupanyone.com. I don't know what public records they had to scour to get their information, but the website seemed to have the age of virtually everyone I looked up, except for one online date who had been born in England.

I'd agreed to meet the Englishman at a local pub for a quick drink. For the first five or maybe it was ten minutes, I was charmed by his accent and good manners. The American Billboard Awards were on the bar TV and Taylor Swift came dancing onto the screen in a pair of shorts. My date stared at the screen, looking pained, and then said, "She's got awfully big thighs, doesn't she?"

I was too startled to answer, and he continued, "She's hippy, too, isn't she. I don't really like hips."

I finally recovered my voice and said, "How about breasts? How do you feel about them?"

He answered that he didn't "mind" breasts, and they could be big or small. The bartendress, who'd been watching the show standing near us, refilled my glass of wine, unasked.

Back to lying about one's age. When I first figured out how to look up people's ages, my mom and I spent a delightful afternoon typing in her friends' and neighbors' names and finding out their ages.

When I got back to my apartment and did my own searches, I no longer felt so delighted. I don't know if it's something in the water in my Florida beachside community, but I was startled to discover that many of my dates had lied about their ages.

Numerous past dates had lied by one or two years, some had lied by several years, and a surprising number of my past dates had lied by five to ten years. I emailed one of my girlfriends and we discovered that a man she was currently corresponding with was lying by an astonishing 18 years.

It is possible that the reason men lie so very much here is because so many people have moved to Sarasota from somewhere else, which makes starting one's new life with a new age apparently too tempting to resist.

Romantic Scams

Astonishingly, it has been estimated that ten percent of the people on internet dating sites are scammers, sex offenders, or criminals.

According to the Internet Crime Report Center, the internet romance scams that were reported to authorities (probably vastly understating the real amount) added up to over eighty-one million dollars in 2013, and forty-seven million of that loss was by women over fifty. The only internet scam with more money lost was auto fraud.

All I have to say about romance scams is this: if a man you are corresponding with online asks you for money, *run like the wind*.

Seriously, run. There's no reason on earth a man you've been emailing with should ask you for money. Here's what to watch out for, straight from the FBI website:

Your online "date" may only be interested in your money if he or she:
– Presses you to leave the dating website you met

through and to communicate using personal email or instant messaging;
- Professes instant feelings of love;
- Sends you a photograph of himself or herself that looks like something from a glamour magazine;
- Claims to be from the U.S. and is traveling or working overseas;
- Makes plans to visit you but is then unable to do so because of a tragic event; or
- Asks for money for a variety of reasons (travel, medical emergencies, hotel bills, hospitals bills for a child or other relative, visas or other official documents, losses from a financial setback or crime victimization).

Another common scam is when a romance scammer pretends to be a member of the American military serving overseas who needs money. One particularly appealing-looking military police officer reported that he'd had a photo he'd posted from Iraq used so many times by scammers that he'd had over 300 women contact him on Facebook who thought they'd been corresponding with him.

A spokesman for the U.S. Army Criminal Investigation Command warned in a written statement:

"We cannot stress enough that people need to stop sending money to persons they meet on the internet and claim to be in the U.S. Military ... If someone asked you out on a first date and before they picked you up they asked you for $3,000 to fix their car to come get you, many people would find that very suspicious and certainly would not give them the money. This is the same thing, except over the Internet."

Sadly, scammers will sometimes take the name of a deceased U.S. soldier to perpetuate their scam.

If a Man Asks You For Money

If a man you've been corresponding with asks you for money, write him back something like this: "*I was just going to ask you for money! You say you need $5,000? I need $10,000! And I need it tomorrow, or I will be kicked out of the state of Iowa.*"

And if he actually sends you money? Well, you may have found yourself a keeper.

The Most Handsome Man on Earth

I had a girlfriend tell me excitedly that the most handsome man on Earth had contacted her on a dating site we both belonged to. At her suggestion, I went online to admire his photo. He was indeed one of the most handsome men I'd ever seen, online or elsewhere. Since I am a naturally suspicious person, I started wondering why the most handsome man on Earth, an architect who supposedly lived in a Tampa suburb, was writing to my girlfriend.

I plugged the most handsome man on Earth's photo into a website called Tineye.com. This free website allows you to upload a photo and then view where else the photo can be found online. And it turned out that the photo was that of a very glamorous, European former pro soccer star.

I informed my girlfriend of my unfortunate finding, hoping she wouldn't think less of me for wondering if the most handsome man on Earth would be writing to her. Thankfully, she took it well, though I think she was a bit sad to say goodbye to her fake glamorous suitor.

My Photos Take a Trip, All on Their Own

I made friends with a man from Match.com who seemed to be completely romantically uninterested in me, but who occasionally asked me to meet him for dinner, apparently so that he could complain about this or that gorgeous women who wasn't writing him back. He always paid for dinner, and he didn't seem to care how much I drank so I usually said yes when he called, I mean, I've spent worse nights out.

He smiled across the table at me one night and said, "So, I see you're on PlentyOfFish now."

I said, "No, I'm not on PlentyOfFish."

He frowned and said, "No, really, how are you liking PlentyOfFish?"

I frowned and I said, "No, really, I'm not on PlentyOfFish."

He said, "Yes, you are."

At this point, I was wishing I had just gone to the grocery store and bought my own bottle of Kendall Jackson Chardonnay, I mean, this was getting ridiculous.

Then my guy friend said, "I just saw your photo on PlentyOfFish last week. I wrote you. I wondered why you didn't write back." Then he got on his phone and showed me my photos on POF, along with a profile name I didn't recognize.

I almost screamed out loud I was so startled. Some mofo had photographed my photos (they were very grainy) and had a fake profile of me in Fort Myers, Florida about one hundred miles away.

I went home and emailed POF and they took the fake profile down the next day. My guy friend kept checking for me periodically and my fake profile didn't reappear on PlentyOfFish, at least not in Fort Myers.

But who knows? Maybe my photos are still out there, luring in unsuspecting men in Omaha and Boise. How could I possibly know? I hope my fake photo person is behaving him or herself with my photos, but I doubt it.

And such are the endless miseries of an online dating life.

11

The Super-Secret Algorithms of Love

"[E]veryone knows that all personality profiling is bullshit."
–Brian Bowman, former v.p., Match.com

Um, What is an Algorithm, Anyway?

Everyone on Earth is now aware that there are magical, mystical "scientific" algorithmic matching systems the online dating sites use to match eager singles of all ages.

Since I didn't know exactly what an algorithm was I decided to look up the definition on Wikipedia, which read as follows: "An algorithm is an effective method expressed as a finite list of well-defined instructions for calculating a function."

I'm not ashamed to admit that after reading the definition above, I remained somewhat confused. I called a math major friend for help and he asked why I wanted to know. When I explained, he said that the online dating sites are using mathematical calculations to feed in information about you to try to figure out who you might get along with. I asked him if he thought that would work well and he paused, for quite a long time. Then he said, "Well, it sure didn't for me!"

My Algo Analysis

I am going to admit right here, right now, that I still don't know what an algorithm is. That being said, I am about to do an "algo-analysis" for the largest dating websites in the United States.

Match

Dan Slater, the journalist who wrote *Love in the Time of Algorithms*, obtained this gem of a quote about Match.com's own view of its matching algorithms from Brian Bowman, a former vice president of Match.com: "When eHarmony took so much market share in the early 2000s, we hired the best science people … It was clear that there was absolutely no validity to personality profiling. But eHarmony was doing a huge marketing push. The good, white-haired doctor was big presence on TV. So we had to offer what he was offering."

Quelle surprise, is all I have to say, about the effectiveness, or lack thereof, of personality profiling. Match, OkCupid, POF, and eHarmony all valiantly attempt to make matches for you, but your viewpoint about the validity of their "matches" depends upon your degree of naiveté about the world and its people. It's really just an endless stream of meaningless matches, something akin to matching white noise.

If you've been on any dating website long enough, you start to suspect that they're just throwing their subscriber base at you in your zip code and age group, and then they start matching you with users in neighboring communities.

Since you are allowed to search through all the profiles on Match and OkCupid and POF, it really doesn't matter if their matching systems work or not. You can happily check out potential dates in all fifty states, which is exactly what some men seem to do.

I once went out with a very sweet man who mentioned that we were lucky the dating website had matched us together or we'd have never met. When I squinted at him quizzically and asked him if he was aware that he could search the site and not just wait passively to be matched, he looked astonished, and then delighted. With a sinking heart, I realized that I had unleashed him on the other women on the website, never to be heard from again.

Enough about Match's matching algorithms, such as they are. It's time to move on to POF.

POF (PlentyOfFish)

POF's famously casual CEO Markus Frind ran POF as its sole employee for the first five years of its existence. (And is now being bought out by the Match Group, with the deal scheduled to close in December of 2015.) If there are any magic matching algorithms going on at POF, they're not Harvard-level, and we'll leave it at that. The POF website itself simply states:

> "Your matches are influenced by a combination of basic search settings and your actions on the site. The system identifies what users you generally search for, as well as a number of other factors in the system when creating your matches. The more searching and general using of the site you do, the better the system can create appropriate matches for you."

I don't think there's a lot of matching wizardry going on at POF, which is a bit of an infamous hookup site. I perused their message boards to check out other users' views of their matches. The male users seemed to be no more pleased with the matching system than the women. One male user complained quite sadly that he was a Christian and wanted kids, and was being matched with women who were neither religious or interested in kids. His theory? Same as mine. The matches were being made basically by gender and zip code. Another male user commented that a random number generator would work better.

POF's best feature, as always, is that it is free.

OkCupid

OkCupid offers up hundreds and hundreds of optional questions that users can answer, and then the Harvard math-major founders toss this information into their magic blender and come up with a matching percentage for you and your fellow users.

So does the Harvard-math-major-matching system work? Well, here's what Christian Rudder of OkCupid told *Salon's* Andrew Leonard in 2014: "But when we describe people as good or bad matches — the truth is for any two people on OkCupid, we just don't know. We're making a guess; our algorithm is a version of a guess."

I would have to agree with Christian Rudder about OkCupid's matching. In one of the first matches in my "quiver," I got a man openly looking for a threesome, which wasn't exactly what I was looking for in a dating companion.

I do think that if you take the time to compare the sometimes-intriguing questions you can choose to answer with those of another user, you can glean some interesting and potentially relevant information.

In Sarasota, Florida however, the men on OkCupid seem to view it as some sort of 70s-style, 'sexual healing' site, so it doesn't really matter who you're matched with. Even Harvard math majors need something to work with to make a match, just like you need the right hair and jaw line for a pixie cut.

eHarmony and Chemistry Do the Matching For You. Isn't That Nice of Them?

Both Chemistry and eHarmony do not allow you to freely roam their websites, but instead pick your matches for you, using their algorithms of love. Quite obviously, their matching systems will be of the utmost importance to your experience on their websites.

Chemistry

I'm going to focus first on Chemistry, which is owned by the Match Group. I'd seen their ads for a long time on Match, but I'd ignored the ads, mistakenly assuming that by "chemistry" they meant "sex," and that it was some sort of offshoot Match sex site.

When I finally looked into it, I admit to some amazement at what I discovered. Apparently, the corporate masters who own Match were concerned about the growing popularity of eHarmony and its algorithms of love. So in 2006, they contacted Helen Fisher, a biological anthropologist, and asked her if she would like to design a magical-mystery-tour formula of love for a new dating website. I mean I'm sure they didn't put it *exactly* like that, but it's probably close.

She said she responded with: "Are you sure you've got the right person? Because I'm an anthropologist. I've spent my life studying why we're all alike, not why we're different."

Maybe it's just me, but that's not a good start. Fisher recounted that she then sat down with some pieces of paper and tried to figure out a formula. Fast forward to the present and Chemistry.com matches subscribers based in part upon their hormonal levels of testosterone, estrogen, serotonin and dopamine. (You can't make this stuff up.)

Here's how it works: if you're decisive and competitive, you must be high in testosterone, and you're labeled a "director." If you're intuitive and empathetic, you're obviously high in estrogen, so you're labeled a "negotiator." If you're curious and adventurous, you're an "explorer" with high levels of dopamine; and if you're traditional and cautious, you're a "builder," who must be high in serotonin.

According to the Chemistry formula, the open-minded explorers go for explorers; the conventional builders go for their fellow traditional builders; and the compassionate negotiators go for the analytical directors, who prefer the negotiators right back.

I don't mean to throw a wrench into what is obviously a smoothly functioning machine, but, um, if "negotiators" who are fueled by estrogen go for "directors" who are fueled by testosterone—and vice versa—wouldn't that logically lead to matching women with men? Which isn't exactly a novel concept.

Enough about Chemistry and hormonal matching. Onward... to eHarmony.

eHarmony

Oh, eHarmony, where do I begin? I mean, really—where? EHarmony claims that it has a secret sauce to match truly compatible people that it has termed "the 29 Dimensions of Compatibility." From eHarmony's website:

> "Out of all the single people you will meet in your life, only a very few would make a great relationship partner for you. Some singles aren't attractive to you. Others aren't ready for a relationship. Of the rest, many are great people who you might enjoy chem-

istry with initially, but they aren't compatible with you in the important ways that make long-term dating and relationships work. That's where eHarmony comes in. By combining the best scientific research with detailed profiling of every member, we screen thousands of single men and single women to bring you only the ones that have the potential to be truly right for you."

Those are some mighty big claims there. When you watch the eHarmony ads, you start to think, "Hey! Maybe if I pay for an expensive monthly subscription or even sign up for the very best deal for a one-year subscription, this magical site and this dear old man will match me with my soul mate!"

eHarmony's founder, Neil Clark Warren, was a marriage counselor for thirty-some years. Apparently he decided after years of counseling that he knew why couples got along and why they didn't, and decided to start a mystical website using his theories.

The eHarmony website lists the dimensions of personality that are part of eHarmony's formula. Included in their algorithm are traits and attributes like character, kindness, dominance, sociability, autonomy, intellect, humor, family status, artistic passion, obstreperousness and appearance.

I admit it. I fell for it. I signed up for a free weekend, hoping to meet a man that truly matched me, on all the dimensions of my personality, except for maybe "obstreperousness," a man carefully chosen just for me. I dutifully filled out the personality test, wondering where it would lead me. And here's what happened: I was matched during the course of the weekend with one of my girlfriends' past boyfriends. When she joined, she got matched with him, too. (They'd met on Match.) Then a third girlfriend joined and she got matched with the same man, too.

Now, if you looked at eHarmony's mix of character traits, you could say that all of us are sociable and basically sane. But at core my girlfriends and I are very different people—too different to have been matched with the same man based upon a magic formula of compatibility.

Just as one small example, one of eHarmony's core traits is physical energy, and I don't particularly like to exercise. If I had to choose an animal that I'm most like, it would be a sloth. I once watched five *Breaking Bad*s in a row, getting up only for wine and restroom breaks. By contrast, my girlfriend who'd dated this man is a dynamo of physical energy, and even owns her own kayak.

Furthermore, spirituality is one of eHarmony's "dimensions," and one of us is very religious, while the others are not.

My personal theory is that eHarmony matched all three of us with the same man because there weren't that many people on eHarmony in Sarasota, and so it made sense to just throw mud on the wall, as it were, and see if something stuck.

NY Times Reporter Tries eHarmony, along with his Wife

A *New York Times* columnist named John Tierney wrote

an interesting article about his time on eHarmony titled "My eHarmony Experiment: Can This Marriage Be Matched?" in which he describes signing up for eHarmony, along with his wife. Tierney had decided to test eHarmony's matching system and see if he and his wife would be matched with each other. They filled out their questionnaires and found that they tested very similarly in most of eHarmony's dimensions of personality.

Of the several dozen matches they both got in the next week or so, they weren't matched up together. So Tierney, being a *New York Times* columnist and thus able to actually call up eHarmony and figure out what the hell is going on, went in to talk to one of eHarmony's top advisors.

During their discussion, the advisor asked Tierney how he and his wife had filled out their preferences for dating others who drink or smoke. Tierney replied that his wife had said that she was open to someone who smoked, though she didn't smoke herself.

According to Tierney, the eHarmony advisor then advised him that user satisfaction was higher if they kept those who would tolerate smokers apart from those who wouldn't.

So that's a portion of the magical "secret sauce"? The secret to a deep emotional compatibility? That John Tierney wasn't open to dating a smoker and that his wife was?

Tierney's wife went back on eHarmony to change her preference to *not* being open to dating a smoker. And Voila! Tierney and his wife still didn't get matched up.

My personal theory as to why the Tierneys weren't matched is that the powers-that-be at eHarmony have to keep their old subscribers happy with new matches, so I assume that they allocate the newbies to the oldies, to keep everyone happy.

So What Do the Academicians Think About Algorithmic Matching?

I'll sum it up in two words: they're skeptical. Okay, I'll add a third word: they're highly skeptical.

Eli Finkel, who co-authored an influential paper analyzing the shortcomings of online dating, was blunt in an interview with the *New York Times's* Nick Bolton: "We, as a scientific community, do not believe that these algorithms work." He continued, "They are a joke, and there is no relationship scientist that takes them seriously as relationship science."

Thomas Bradbury, a clinical psychology professor and relationship researcher at UCLA, was quoted in an *LA Weekly* article about online dating's matching formulas calling out Chemistry's matching methods as "*almost crazy.*" In the same article, fellow UCLA professor and relationship researcher Benjamin Karney describes eHarmony's lofty soulmate matching as "*a pretty drastic claim.*" Karney says that their advertising claim should really be something more like: "'*We've screened out the freaks.' That could be their tagline — eHarmony: No freaks here.*"

Academic social scientists have long suggested that eHarmony run experiments comparing groups matched using their algorithms with control groups and that the results are published in a peer-reviewed academic journal.

When and if that happens, I'll be sure to let you know.

So Why Don't the Algos Work?

You might ask, why is it that the academicians are so skeptical about the online dating websites' algorithmic matching formulas?

It turns out that social scientists have come to the conclusion that personality similarities really don't have a thing to do with relationship happiness. One study that pooled data from 313 other studies showed that the relationship between personality attributes and relationship satisfaction in existing relationships was—believe it or not—about zero.

So the possibility of devising a formula feeding in the dry information from an online dating profile that could successfully predict whether two people will fall in love is also… about zero.

Instead, the years of studies have found that it's the way two people interact once they've met—their personal communication styles; their relationships with friends and family; their sexual compatibility; their reactions to the outside world, to the stressors of life and within their relationship—that affects a couple's relationship satisfaction.

Psychologist Robert Epstein, former editor of *Psychology Today*, went so far as to write in *Scientific American*:

> "I have been a researcher for about 30 years and a test designer for nearly half those years. When I see extravagant ads for online tests that promise to find

people a soul mate, I find myself asking, "How on earth could such a test exist? The truth is, it doesn't."

eHarmony, Redux

Oh, eHarmony, you didn't think I was finished with you yet, did you? Let me give one more personal example about eHarmony and my dating life.

It's time to make another rather embarrassing confession. Even after my unproductive free weekend on eHarmony, I paid up to join the site a few months later. What can I say? Those are some damn good ads. I excused my disappointing "free communication weekend" experience, thinking perhaps that you had to join to get the full eHarmony experience.

I was immediately matched with a man who turned out to be lying about his age by 7 years. (And who was only visiting a relative in our metropolitan area, and actually lived in St. Louis, Missouri.)

I met another man for drinks and appetizers. As we sipped our wine, he told me his theory about Medicare reform, which was that the majority of seniors should not receive any benefits, even if they had to sell their homes to fund their medical care.

Any politician who instituted this reform in Florida would be railroaded from office but there was no point in arguing so I munched on my tuna tartare and nodded politely.

He must have sensed that I wasn't falling for him or his Medicare reform theories and so—in the middle of dinner—he abruptly called the waitress over for the check. He paid his part and left me drinking my almost full glass of Conundrum Chardonnay, which soothed me as I finished my meal, alone.

So it turned out that eHarmony's magical formula envisioned me with a liar and an extremely rude socialist.

Within the first week of my eHarmony subscription, I received matches from Atlanta, Alabama, and North Carolina, in addition to cities all over Florida.

I don't consider myself to be particularly sentimental. If you tell me that my perfect match is in Henderson, North Carolina, I'm like Rhett Butler with Scarlett: I don't give a damn.

I soon deactivated myself from the site, never to return.

My Own Magical and "Scientific" Theory

It doesn't matter who they match you up with. *This* is who you're gonna meet:

The Talker

I spent my entire life before online dating assuming that women talked more than men. I can talk so much that I could be hired out to stand in as a professional filibusterer in the Senate. You need someone to talk all night so a bill can't be passed in Congress? Sign me on.

But I have had more dates than I could count when I just listened and nodded and was cut off whenever I tried to add much to the conversation. Therapists get paid a lot of money to listen to someone else talk non-stop for an hour while they nod politely and interject sympathetic comments. Dates should not be regarded as inexpensive therapy sessions, though many men seem to view them as such.

On a side note, why are all the late night talk show hosts men? Here's who can carry on a good conversation: women.

The Angry Divorced Guy

You've barely taken two sips of your Pinot Grigio and the angry divorced guy starts in on his ex-wife, who's invariably "crazy." Here's how to shut him up: ask him to name the exact diagnostic category his ex-wife was diagnosed with. Another good question to head him off at the pass: what did he do to try to help her?

The angry divorced guys don't seem to realize what we women all know: if the ex-wife acted crazy, or was depressed, or caused "drama," the likelihood is high that the man sitting across the table had some part in it.

The Weirdo

I met a man for coffee whose profile said that he went to Brown. We sat outside at my neighborhood Starbucks and he spent most of the date nervously watching cars going by in the parking lot. He explained that he thought he kept seeing his ex-wife's car circle past, though she currently lived in a suburb of Philadelphia, which was approximately one thousand miles away.

The next day he texted me asking if I wanted to go shopping

with him. I checked his profile again to try to figure out where I'd gone wrong and he'd already changed his college to the Naval Academy.

The Creep

Creeps are everywhere on the online sites. Even those cute Harvard math geeks who started OkCupid seem a little chastened at the Pandora's box of freaks they've unleashed upon the world.

I once went out boating on the Gulf of Mexico on a first date with a nice-looking lawyer. We were within sight of a ritzy Longboat Key beachside resort filled with cabanas and beachgoers when he suggested that we were far enough from shore to safely sunbathe nude. I still remember my astonishment, as I was currently wearing a long-sleeved shirt, a big hat, boat shorts, and three kinds of sunscreen to protect my Scandinavian skin. (Oh! And I'd just met him an hour and a half before.)

When I demurred, he told me sternly that he was the captain and I was the first mate and that if I didn't obey him, I could get thrown overboard. I'm a good swimmer and I was tempted to go overboard on my own, but the water was fairly choppy so I decided to feign sea sickness and I was eventually returned home, none the worse for the wear.

When my mother asked how my date was, I said I didn't like his dog and that answer seemed to suffice, as always.

The Guy Who is Too Old for You

It doesn't matter how old you are when you get on an online dating site—there's always a man fifteen or twenty years older than you who tries to convince you how great a match he'd be for you.

A doctor who'd given some of his residency information in his profile once emailed me. I tried punching it into Google and after a long search I found a man who'd had the same medical residency sequence and the same photo. I plugged his name into Lookupanyone.com and voila! He was 20 years older than he'd claimed. That took some big giant balls, and I gave him credit for that when I wrote him politely declining our upcoming date.

My mother used to ask why men wanted so desperately to date younger women. I knew why, but I never told her. Men want the youngest-looking ass they can get and it's no more complicated than that. But that doesn't make it any easier to take. I don't particularly like old ass, either, but you don't see me lying about my age.

The Teary-Eyed Widower

I went out for dinner with a widower who told me that he would "never get over the loss of his wife." That's a shame, but it's not exactly in the top one hundred traits I'm looking for in a man.

As it turned out, his wife had died a mere two months before and his therapist thought it was a good idea for him to get out. (His dates' feelings, apparently, were unimportant.) My widower date spent the entire dinner talking loudly about his wife. He met his wife at a James Taylor concert! His wife took pastry courses! In France! It sounded to the next table like I was a put-upon mistress who had to sleep with this man *and* listen to him talk about his wife.

I later emailed the widower telling him about a widower's website I'd found that was filled with advice for fellow widowers. (Which makes it quite clear to bereaved men that there can only be two people in a relationship. And that you gotta say "my late wife.") What can I say? Regardless of what you might have heard, I'm a helper.

The Cheap Guy

An engineer I dated a few times came over to pick me up for a movie and when I opened the door he was holding a big plastic bag filled with popcorn that he wanted me to sneak into the movie for him. I tried to explain that a large bag of popcorn didn't fit under my current outfit, which consisted of a slim-fitting shirt and jeans.

Unfazed, he looked through my coat closet, found a knitted cardigan sweater, and told me to put that on. Before we left, he opened my refrigerator and tried to talk me into shoving a cupcake into my purse for my own snack. Admittedly, the food is overpriced at the movies. But still. A cupcake in a purse is not a good thing.

The movie attendants kindly let me through, but I didn't feel so kindly toward my frugal date. If he wanted cheap popcorn so badly, he should have walked into the movie theater with a big cyst-like lump on his side, instead of me.

Here's what I think: if you won't pay up for the pop-corn, don't ask a woman to the movies.

Dionysus, The Love Guy

I am of the opinion that some men switch between porn and online dating sites. You know the type: their profiles are written with one hand on the keyboard and one on their dick. Their online moniker reads something like "AmorousJoe69." They want "sensuous, adventurous vixens." They've got "slow hands" and love "Sundays in bed with you and the *New York Times*." Their profiles include gems like: "Love to lick and be licked."

I've got a new flash for all you Love Guys out there: We get it. You're interested in a good sex life. The women who aren't interested in sex aren't online—they're busy gardening and acting in community theater productions. Those women are smarter than I am, and make better use of their free time, too. Get your hand out of your pants and write a normal profile.

The Instant Soul Mate

This man wants to spend his every waking moment with the woman of his dreams, just as soon as he meets her. I try very hard not to meet anyone who expresses an interest in accompanying me to the grocery store, but I still have gone on a surprising number of dates where the man has decided, during the date, or shortly thereafter, that fate has brought us together.

I once had a man insist that we were meant for each other and that we take our profiles down—before we had met.

It can't be because of my personality, which one of my cousins said reminded her of Kathy Griffin's, so apparently there are some men out there who are ready to settle down with virtually any woman who agrees to meet them for a date. I think perhaps it's a function of testosterone, too, like they're peeing near you and marking their territory.

The Shining Star

You know this type, too, if you've been online dating long enough. There are certain men—based on their looks, social status, high-profile job, whatever—who know that they can get virtually any woman on a dating website to meet for a drink.

You also know that they're trouble in a bubble. These men are gathering scalps while patiently waiting for Elisha Cuthbert, or Emma Stone, or Sharon Stone, or whatever age range they happen to be in to join the online dating parade, just like Martha Stewart did.

One of the most desirable men on Match in Sarasota asked me to meet him for lunch and, surprised but flattered, I agreed. I ran into him in the parking lot as I parked my Honda and he parked his expensive sports car. After talking nonstop about himself the entire meal, other than to ask me repeatedly what actress I thought I was most like (answer: none), he asked me what actor I thought *he* was most like.

After some very large dropped hints about the actor he resembled always playing a good guy everyone admired, I correctly guessed Tom Hanks. He texted me later that night while I was out with my parents for dinner, asking if I'd thought of an actress I resembled yet. My mom, deep into her vodka martini, suggested Goldie Hawn and Cate Blanchett. When I protested that Goldie and Cate were a ridiculous combination, she said that it was a ridiculous question and deserved an equally ridiculous reply. I texted faux Tom Hanks back with my Cate/Goldie combination and assumed I was done with him.

He texted me a couple days later and asked me to come over in the middle of the afternoon to watch a movie starring, who else? Cate Blanchett. Even women in Afghanistan know what a movie date on the sofa means and I texted him back that Rita Wilson wouldn't approve. I never heard from him again but I see him out and about occasionally, usually with arm candy draped on his faux Tom Hanks' arm, looking pleased with himself.

The Player

I wrote an entire chapter of this book about players, and also my theory that players are either Machiavellians, psychopaths, narcissists, or all three. Oh! And that they're assholes, too. Clearly, these men hold a spot near and dear to my heart.

The online dating websites are their sandboxes, and we're the discarded toys by the side of the box. May they all go to Hell, where hopefully wild dogs will tear out their intestines throughout eternity.

12

Ageism and Men

"When a man of 40 falls in love with a girl of 20, it
isn't her youth he is seeking but his own."
–Lenore Coffee, author

"Men can't see their own aging bodies. And the
more money they have, the dimmer the mirror."
–My mother

Look! I'm Invisible!

If you're under 30, you can skip this chapter. For the rest of
you, well, welcome to my sinking ship.

When the ageism of men mixes with the endless selection
of younger women offered up on the online dating sites, the
combination is toxic. The men get confused and the women
get fucked up the—well, pick an orifice. Any orifice will do.
I'm going to pick the ear. Online dating for a woman over the
age of 30 is like getting fucked in the ear. I know that sounds
ridiculous, but so is online dating for a woman past a certain
age.

To my knowledge, Christie Brinkley has never online dated but I'm pulling her into this discussion anyway. She said in an interview with *Entertainment Tonight* that she feels invisible to men her own age. And if Christie Brinkley is invisible to men her age, then the rest of us are even more invisible, if that's possible. It's like we're wearing Harry Potter's magic cloak of invisibility.

Men's natural tendency toward ageism becomes an exponentially larger problem while online dating, since men can search in their desired younger age range and not even see women their own age. After I'd been on and off Match for a year, I contacted a man my own age who I'd seen on the dating website for months. He assumed that I'd just joined the site because—of course!—he'd never seen my photo, because he'd never searched for a woman his own age.

It goes without saying but I'll say it anyway: the same woman a man might miss on an online search for a younger woman could be attractive to him in real life. And the researchers agree. As a recent study pointed out:

> "When potential dating partners first meet one another in a traditional setting such as a bar, specific attributes such as exact age are not readily apparent. However, in the online dating environment, individuals chose somewhat arbitrary cut-offs as their search criteria and acknowledged that this might preclude opportunities to meet potential good matches."

Let's see what 'ole Christian Rudder has to say about ageism.

In his book *Dataclysm,* he disclosed that women on OkCupid seem to find men their age attractive. (Or at least keep messaging them.) In comparison, his analysis of male messaging trends showed that as men age they begin to message fewer and fewer women their own age. In fact, Rudder found that 35-year-old men on OkCupid seldom message women over the age of 29. By age 48, he writes, "men are nearly twice as sought after as women." Sounding a bit regretful for us, he writes, "Women want men to age with them. And men will always head to youth."

Yep, that brought up a little bile up in my throat, too.

POF founder Markus Frind ended up sending a mass email to his user base banning men—um, I mean POF members—from contacting other members outside a 14-year age range from their own. In the email, he noted that there was really no reason for a 50-year-old man to be contacting an 18-year-old woman, which I would venture to guess most people would agree with, except for perhaps 50-year-old men.

The Puzzle of Men and Uber-Ageism

One warm summer night, I met a man at one of my favorite restaurants which overlooked a local marina. He had an interesting profile, with a great list of books he'd read, including one of my favorites. His desired age range ended four years below his own age but I was safely younger so I'd limboed into his view on the online dating site.

In my written profile, I'd clearly stated, "If you won't date someone your own age, I won't, either," but apparently he hadn't read that far and I generally didn't follow my own rule anyway, or I wouldn't have had anyone to go out with.

My date and I ran into each other at the marina, and as we admired the million-dollar yachts, I remember being surprised that someone who wouldn't date a woman his own age looked like he wasn't aging any too well. Let's just say he probably should budget for some facial filler and leave it at that.

Once we'd sat down and ordered a drink, in my endless search to figure out how men's brains work, I decided to ask my date about his age-range preference.

I said that I'd noticed he wouldn't date anyone his own age, and then I asked him what he'd do if the hottest woman from his high school class found him on Facebook and wanted to get together.

He smirked as he answered, "I went to an all-boys high school."

Oh, men are so endlessly amusing, aren't they? Since I'm sometimes like a dog with a bone, I named a couple beautiful actresses his age and asked him if he'd date them. He smirked again as he declared that he found younger women more attractive. Then he declared that he was "draconian" about the way a woman's body looked. He said it really casually, like it was a Constitutional right: "I have a right to bear arms and to demand that a woman's body be smoking hot. Despite my sagging jowls."

The really amusing part of this story is that when I later found the website Lookupanyone.com where I could look up his age, I discovered that he was really three years older than he said he was. So he wouldn't go out with women his own age, or his fake younger age, either.

This raises the following two questions: Can men not see themselves? Can they not make a realistic assessment of their own worth and their prospects and adjust their expectations accordingly? I'll answer the quiz questions for you: no.

The astute online dating coach Evan Marc Katz (whom I should have hired during my online dating sojourn, probably sometime during the first week), commented on older male daters on his website, Evanmarckatz.com:

> "Older men have a huge blind spot when it comes to age. They refuse to even consider women their own age, even if she's fit and attractive. Worse, they're hypocritical about it, because they don't understand why the vast majority of younger women won't go for them."

Hey, Maybe We Should Just Date Older Men

I have heard it suggested that women in their thirties should date men in their forties, women in their forties should date men in their fifties; and so on, to the grave. Like, if that's what men want, what's so bad about it? Why don't we just give in to the inevitable?

Here's why: **I want to date someone my own age.** (Note the bold lettering? This subject gets me a little hot under the collar. Like Jody Arias hot under the collar.) Imagine if someone told all the men in the world that they could only date women ten years older. They would be sad, and mad. No, seriously, they would burn down the world. It would actually blow up, like an exploding star that briefly outshines the sun.

Let's Talk about Men Over Fifty

According to the CEO of the Match group, the fastest growing group of online daters is people over the age of 50. And men over fifty take the cake for their ageism. Studies have shown that as men age, they start preferring women with even larger age gaps from their own, which takes a bit of nerve, considering. One study found that men in their fifties prefer women who are ten to twenty years younger.

I don't quite understand what men in their fifties, sixties and seventies think they can bring to the table when writing women more than fifteen years their junior.

One beautiful sunny morning, I met a recently divorced fifty-year-old man at my favorite coffee shop. As I munched an excellent M&M cookie along with my vanilla latte, he told me that he was surprised that a woman fifteen years younger had contacted him and seemed very interested in going out with him. And that even *younger* women had been contacting him.

He told me sort of proudly; like he was a stud horse whose sperm was so valuable that he could be hired out for good money to continue his bloodline.

I was feeling feisty from all the sugar and I said, "They're probably pros, or women with money troubles." He blinked twice at me; first looking confused, then slightly offended.

He actually called me again for a date, slightly redeeming

himself, but I remain amazed at men's egos. Most women are fairly creeped out when someone fifteen years older writes to them. Thirty-year-old women (who aren't pros or don't have money problems) don't want to hear from 45-year-old men. Fifty-year-old women (who can no longer be pros so those who don't have money problems) don't want to hear from 65-year-old men. *But the men keep writing to them.* They're always full of arguments why they want a younger woman: They "relate better" to younger people. Everyone tells them they look young for their age. And then there's their favorite argument: They're "too active" for women their age. (Which always made me feel vaguely nauseated, for some reason.)

Do you ever wish you could put a curse on people? I do. All the time. (I wish more stores carried voodoo dolls.) And one group of people I'd like to curse is men who cannot see women their own age as attractive. Or who think that considerably younger women will date them for any but the most mercenary of reasons.

Yes, George Clooney snagged the long-legged, much younger Amal Alamuddin, but he's George Clooney. Clint Eastwood can date and marry all the younger women he wants. All I'm saying is if a man wants a much younger woman, he'd better bring something extra special to the dating table. Most men don't.

I remember watching a movie with one of my past dates—remember the man I threw up on? Yep, it was him. Anyway, shortly before the night I threw up on him, we were watching a movie on Netflix that featured both Catherine Keener and Amanda Peet (who is thirteen years younger than Catherine).

My date, who was 53, squinted at the on-screen 49-year-old Catherine Keener like he was pained by what he saw, and said, "She looks really old." I didn't think Catherine looked old at all and in fact I thought she looked lovely, but I don't usually talk during movies so I kept my mouth shut.

A few minutes later, the 36-year-old Amanda Peet came on the screen and he brightened. He turned to me and said, "Who is she? She's really cute."

What I wanted to say was, "I don't know why you give a fuck what her name is because she doesn't give a fuck about yours," but I just said, "Amanda Peet" and kept drinking my wine, which soothed me, as always.

Top Ten Reasons Online Dating Doesn't Work for Women Over Thirty

1. Men who are in great shape want younger women.
2. Men with man boobs and gelatinous stomachs want younger women.
3. Rich men want younger women.
4. Men who want to meet for coffee and then come late so you've already paid for your own coffee want younger women.
5. Men with great jobs want younger women.
6. Men who are "self-employed" and live in RVs want younger women.
7. Hot men want younger women.
8. Men who are not hot want younger women. Oddly, they seem to want them even more.

9. Men in their 30s through their 90s want younger women.
10. Men in the grave want younger crypt keepers and graveyard attendants.

13

The Ads, The Endless Ads

The big online dating websites spent $214 million for advertising in just the first five months of 2014, many of which were on Bravo, my favorite TV station. I saw an ad for Match just the other night, while I was watching *Below Deck,* the Bravo show about a young crew on a yacht-for-hire, which made me want to rent the yacht and order the plucky, overworked staff to fix me pizza and piña coladas in the middle of the night.

In Match's ad, an attractive woman is standing in the street talking to a man who seems to have stopped her for the sole purpose of asking how she planned to meet her next date. She looks a bit confused, just like she is being paid to do, and then she says something like, "Um, the grocery store? A party?" (I was drinking wine so I don't remember exactly what she said or how she came to be talking to this man but you get the idea.)

Anyway, the man in the ad then asks in quite a derisive tone how that's going for her. As if it would be impossible to meet someone naturally, without the help of an online dating company and preferably one of the Match group's dating websites, whose division revenue in 2014 was $836,500,000.

I went to Match's 2014 *"Match Fact Sheet"* (available on their corporate website), and found the following claim: "People who join Match are 3x's more likely to meet find [sic] a relationship than people who don't."

Um, where did they get this statistic? Or the idea that one *has* to join an online dating site to meet someone?

In truth, according to the 2014 Pew Report, "Even among Americans who have been with their spouse or partner for five years or less, fully 88% say that they met their partner offline–without the help of a dating site."

Well, what do you know?! Despite the hard line sell of the online dating industry, people do manage to meet and mingle, every day, without their help.

If you go to any of the dating websites, the hard sell becomes even more frantic, with claims about their websites' messages and conversations and relationships and marriages.

What the dating websites don't mention are the 7.3 million unanswered emails; the 5.6 million mediocre coffee dates; the 4.7 million interminably dull drink dates; the 3.4 million micro-relationships that went nowhere; and the 1.2 million utter relationship disasters that emanated from their sites.

Where'd I get those stats? Out of my ass, just like where the dating websites get theirs.

The Odds of Finding a Fiancée... Are Low

The most interesting of all the OkCupid blog posts was a *deleted* post from 2010 entitled "Why You Should Never Pay For Online Dating." (Which still easily pops up on a Google search.) Christian Rudder fed in the available data about eHarmony's subscriber base numbers and their claimed number of marriages and then after doing a bunch of Harvard-math-major calculations he estimated eHarmony's marriage rate of 6.2 percent, with a corresponding non-marriage rate of 93.8 percent. He added, with a bit of Harvard whimsy, "Those people paid an average of $190 each for a personality quiz."

Rudder also attempted to calculate Match's marriage rates in his now-deleted blog post. Rudder used the numbers supplied by Match on their website and press kit, and figured out that there were roughly 5,000 marriages per 1.3 million Match subscribers, which worked out to a marriage rate of .36 percent. In case you've been drinking while reading, note the decimal placement. That's a less than one percent marriage rate, according to Rudder.

A year after Rudder's 2010 blog post, the company that owns Match bought OkCupid for 90 million dollars, and the blog post *"Why You Should Never Pay for Online Dating"* was promptly deleted. In a 2011 article in the *New York Observer* by Adrianne Jeffries, OkCupid's CEO Sam Yagan rapidly back-pedaled away from the deleted blog post: "In general the totality of data that we have become exposed to leads us to believe that yes, the subscription sites are probably more successful than the post made them out to be."

"Probably more successful." Not exactly a ringing endorsement. If OkCupid were my website and it was bought by Match for 90 million, I would have denied the very existence of the blog post "Why You Should Never Pay for Online Dating," just like Area 51 and possible alien abductions.

I decided to make my own attempt to figure out how many marriages there are per subscriber at Match. I mean, I graduated from a Southern party school, I can do math, too. I went to Match's corporate website and checked their 2014 press kit, but it no longer gives an exact number for marriages per day—or week or year for that matter—that result from their dating service.

Apparently Match.com stopped attempting to supply marriage stats after OkCupid's 2010 blog post, and after a 2009 *Wall Street Journal* article by 'The Numbers Guy' Carl Bialik revealed a blog writer in the online dating industry had crunched the same numbers and figured that it would take 1,369 Match.com dates to get married.

Even to me, that's a lot of dates.

The information in Match's 2014 'fact sheet' now reads: "Match is responsible for more dates, relationships and marriages than any other site. (2x more relationships/marriages than the next competitor.)"

First of all, to whoever put the Match.com "fact sheet" together: Please do not throw relationships *and* marriages *and* dates together. It's not very helpful information, mathematically speaking.

Second of all, if Match is bragging in their "*relationships*" category about mine with the Coach-shoe-obsessed man, or in their "*dates*" category about mine with a biking enthusiast with whom I argued about how many feet a passing driver should give to a biker (should I drive my car into oncoming traffic? I think not), well, all I have to say to Match is: thanks for the memories.

Online Dating Website Membership Figures—Fact or Fiction?

I decided to open a spicy red Zinfandel before trying to figure out the online dating websites' membership numbers. For instance, if a dating website claims 3 million members, does that mean that all 3 million are available, right now, on their site? How many members are *active* versus *inactive*?

It turns out that the big dating websites, and probably the small ones, too, count both active and inactive profiles in their membership counts.

On Match, you're 'inactive' but still counted if you post a profile but you haven't yet subscribed, so you can't send or receive email. You're also 'inactive' if you subscribe and then later cancel your subscription without specifying that your profile be hidden.

What many people with profiles up on Match don't realize is that if you don't actively 'hide' your profile, it could remain on the website for all time. Zombies could take over the world and your fucking profile would still be up on Match.com.

It turns out that we know more about life in North Korea than we know about the exact number of active versus inactive profiles on Match. In his book *Love in the Time of Algorithms*, Slater reports: "According to several former Match employees, the majority of 'new profiles' seen by users in their search results belong to people who haven't paid and therefore cannot respond."

When queried on that subject, Match's current head of

product told Slater that the mix of paid versus free members in searches wasn't something they tracked at Match.

After pouring myself another glass of Zin, I found a 2010 lawsuit against Match on this very matter. A group of plaintiffs filed a class action against Match.com and its corporate over-lord, IAC, alleging that Match.com breached "its covenant of good faith and fair dealing" and that "well over half of the pro-files on its site belong to inactive members."

In 2012, a Texas judge ruled *against* the plaintiffs and *for* Match, but not for the reasons you would assume.

The judge ruled that: "There is nothing in the [Customer] Agreement that obligates Match.com to conduct its services using only current or 'active' profiles."

Further, he ruled that Match had no obligation to "vet, update the website content [or] verify the accuracy of all pro-files submitted..." citing the many disclaimers on Match's website as a basis for his decision.

In other words, legally speaking, inactive or false profiles aren't Match's problem. They're ours.

I hope the good judge has to online date some day and that's all I have to say about that.

Where's the FTC?

Academicians have urged for years that the Federal Trade Commission regulate the online dating companies—just like they do for other consumer products in the U.S.

The FTC sues companies—all the time!—for making advertising claims that are not substantiated by scientific evidence. A couple lingerie companies just got sued for claiming that their caffeine-infused shape-wear reduced cellulite. Then they had to pay a bunch of money and the government refunded it to the consumers who apparently still had cellulite.

But FTC consumer protection over advertising seemingly does not apply to the online dating companies. Nope, they've danced along, unregulated, for years.

If there were a glowing testimonial on a hypothetical vitamin company website from a consumer claiming that she took the company's vitamins and her hair now looked like she had hair extensions, the vitamin website would be required to 1) substantiate these claims, and 2) place a statement near that testimonial that said something like "Results not typical," or even "Notice: These testimonials do not prove our product works. You should not expect to have similar results."

I went to an advertising industry website and viewed some of the Match.com ads available to watch on their site. In many of the Match.com ads, random attractive people are stopped in the street by a man in a suit who asks them if they know someone who has been on Match. And then the random people admit that they know someone—and that person got engaged! Or they went to their wedding! Or their mom found someone! Or their ex! And then the man in the suit acts like the person in the ad is the stupidest person on Earth not to be on Match, too.

Stupider than people who get stuck in doggie doors. Stupider than people who walk along railroad track bridges to take photos and then get hit by a train. Stupider than my spending two months diligently watering two fake plants left on my lanai by the last tenant in my apartment.

But the FTC doesn't require that Match (or any other online dating company) insert a statement that these results might not be typical. Nope, the FTC just... lets it go. I hope the members of the FTC have to online date someday, and that's all I have to say about that.

Who Cares Which Website has the Most Marriages? They do!

Believe it or not, the online dating companies have actually filed claims against each other with the advertising division of the Better Business Bureau. Match filed a claim against eHarmony in 2013 when eHarmony put out this press release: "eHarmony Ranks #1 for Most Online Marriages and Marital Satisfaction in Groundbreaking Marriage Data Published in Proceedings of the National Academy of Sciences (PNAS)* eHarmony Also Has the Lowest Divorce Rate."

The upshot was that in 2014 the National Advertising Division recommended the following: "eHarmony, Inc., discontinue certain "#1" advertising claims for the company's dating website, eHarmony.com, including "#1 Most Marriages," "#1 Most Enduring Marriages," and "#1 Most Satisfying Marriages."

The NAD determined that eHarmony's numbers were too close to Match's to claim any of the above, and that the co-authors of eHarmony's primary study included a former director of eHarmony Laboratories and also a scientific advisor to eHarmony.

In response, eHarmony "respectfully" disagreed with NAD's analysis but agreed to "take NAD's recommendations into consideration in our future advertising."

Sigh. It wasn't guidance from the federal government—instead, it was an advertising industry self-regulatory body—but it's a start.

So, Do the Dating Websites Work as Well as Advertised, or Not?

Here's my vote: Noooooo! But if you don't want to believe someone who's already had half a bottle of Zinfandel, let's hear from the esteemed—and I am assuming not tipsy—professors who co-authored "Online Dating: A Critical Analysis from the Perspective of Psychological Science":

> "These costs in time and money are warranted if online dating actually provides improved, cost-effective access to successful romantic relationships. If such evidence is lacking, however, then people seeking romantic partners may be wasting significant time and money that they could direct toward more productive activities."

I came up with the following list of "more productive activities" than online dating:

Ten Better Uses of Time Than Online Dating

1. Read the Norwegian Book Clubs' top one hundred books of all time.
2. Kamikaze sky-diving. Throw parachute out of airplane, jump out after it.
3. Hot, or cold yoga.
4. Organize the sweaters in your closet into neat columns by color and also color weight.
5. Guess which singer Kanye will insult next at an awards show. Then guess the name of Kim and Kanye's next child.
6. Hike the same mountains as Reese did in *Wild*, but with better boots.
7. Bleach your eyebrows, then draw them back in like Cara Delevingne's.
8. Learn to make beer. Start own micro-brewery.
9. Buy an ant farm for a starter pet.
10. Anything else.

14

A Dizzying Number of Dates

The concept of going out with so many people in such a short period of time is entirely new to the history of the world. Before the advent of online dating, even famous actors and slimy politicians couldn't conjure up three or four dates a week, every week.

I love coffee so much that I look forward to getting out of bed in the morning just to have that first sip, but it got to the point that I dreaded another coffee date spent exchanging banal educational and background information, even if it gave me the chance to drink a vanilla latte, or even a Starbucks white chocolate mocha.

When I went out to eat with my parents, my mother would ask me who I knew in the restaurant, as if I had gone on so many dates that I must know someone I'd dated wherever we went. (I didn't.)

One fine sunny morning I went out to get the mail and opened an envelope from the county government notifying me of jury duty in a few weeks.

I popped out of bed the morning of my jury duty, fixed a to-go coffee with plenty of vanilla creamer and drove off, wondering what was in store for me. Once I got to the courthouse, I checked in and settled onto a plastic chair in a large waiting room filled with other potential jurors. Every once in a while they'd call out about fifteen names and those people would line up and disappear.

Then they started calling name after name to line up. I'd say almost a hundred of us were lined up and then ushered into a spacious courtroom, where we were directed to sit in on rows of wooden benches. I couldn't really see the front of the room and I started chatting with the women sitting next to me.

The stern-looking judge came out and introduced himself. He explained that it was a capital murder case, and that it was going to take some time to choose the jurors for such a big case.

He then asked the prosecutors and the defense attorneys to stand up, and he introduced them to the court. Much to my surprise, up at the front, looking serious, there stood one of my past online dates—the handsome prosecutor.

I leaned over and told the women next to me my predicament. They thought it was hilarious, and also that I'd get to go home soon.

The judge looked over the packed courtroom and asked if anyone knew any of the prosecutors or defense attorneys, or the defendant.

A couple people in the courtroom raised their hands, and after the woman next to me poked me, I raised my hand a couple inches, too.

The judge went around the room asking the people with raised hands how they knew the attorneys who would be handling the case. A couple people worked in county government or had spouses who did and they'd interacted with some of the attorneys. The answers were quick and run-of-the-mill and no one in the courtroom was really paying any attention.

When it got to be my turn, I cleared my throat and said quickly that I was friends with the prosecutor, which I hoped would be enough of an explanation.

The judge smiled at me and said, "So, do you have kids who play with each other?" At this point, everyone in the packed courtroom turned to stare at me.

I began to get kind of nervous, and that's never good. I said, "Well, um, no, we're *friends*." I tried to emphasize the word 'friends' so the judge would quit asking me questions and everyone would quit staring at me, including the creepy defendant, who was accused of killing his wife.

So the judge says, "What do you mean, friends?" I'm not making this up. The judge really wasn't going to let this rest until he knew exactly how the prosecutor and I knew each other.

So I said, sort of desperately, "We dated. We went on dates." My voice must have sounded really plaintive because the entire courtroom cracked up, including the judge and the prosecutor. Even the cops were smiling over at me. Apparently "We dated," is not an answer they hear every day during jury voire dire.

So the judge looks at me and says, "Is there any reason you think you couldn't be an impartial juror in this case?"

I quickly replied "No" to his question and thankfully he moved on.

At our first restroom break I went into the county court-room's very large women's restroom. Most of my fellow female jurors seemed to have crowded themselves into the eight-stall bathroom.

As I was washing my hands, a woman who'd been sitting two rows ahead of me in the courtroom smilingly turned to me and said loudly, "So, did you fuck him?"

All the women in the crowded restroom stared at me curiously and I assured everyone that I hadn't and quickly left the restroom.

A cop standing at the door to the courtroom stared at me as I approached the door to re-enter the courtroom. As I passed him he said, leeringly, "So, you like prosecutors, huh?"

I assured him that I didn't and sank back into my assigned seat on the hard wooden bench, wondering how I had became the slut of the courtroom, despite having had only two dates with the handsome prosecutor, neither of which involved sex.

I had to stay the entire day in that courtroom until finally a group of jurors were chosen for the big murder trial, which the newspapers later avidly covered. I ran into the greatly amused prosecutor as I was leaving the courthouse with the two women whom I sat next to all day. He invited us all out for a drink and so we joined him. Over our drinks, he revealed that he'd put my name in as one of his jury choices but that the defense attorney had struck my name, which seemed fair, considering.

I'm declaring a new, official rule of online dating. If you get called to jury duty and you've dated anyone in that courtroom, you've online dated long enough.

15

Girlfriends are Great

One night in the middle of my online dating life, I sat staring at my computer screen, studying a profile on the screen. Well-educated, attractive, with interesting hobbies and a full life—why not go for it?

I hesitated, and then pressed send. I stared at my computer, fully expecting an irate message from the Match overlords, or even a cancellation of my subscription rights. I'd just messaged a woman! I mean, not a 'woman looking for a woman,' but a 'woman looking for a man.'

Let me back up for a minute. I'd online dated previously in Atlanta, Georgia where I'd moved to start up a food business that folded after a year. I usually hung out with my fellow chefs from the commercial kitchen where we all rented space, and dating wasn't at the top of my priority list.

I'd moved to Sarasota when the food business failed and signed up to online date again. After a couple of bad dates under my belt, I'd decided that what I needed in my new hometown were some girlfriends to dish with. Like Carrie, Samantha, Miranda, and Charlotte.

So I switched my search function to look for women. Onto my screen popped the women who'd been vying with me for the attention of the men in Sarasota, and Tampa and St. Petersburg, too.

As I wrote my email to my chosen group of Match women, I carefully crafted it to make clear that I was a woman who liked men who thought it might be fun to get together for a drink at an upscale beachside restaurant and compare dating notes.

Soon, the replies came rolling in. Women are very polite; much more so than men. Most of the women I'd written to wrote back that they'd be "traveling" or "out of town," but they thanked me for the invitation and told me to let them know if I planned another get-together again. A few women joked that they'd thought I was writing them for a date and had been afraid to read the email!

Three brave women replied and said they'd love to come, and would see me at the restaurant on the suggested night.

A week later, I showed up at the restaurant and one of my chosen girlfriends, a lawyer, was already sitting at the bar drinking a chocolate martini, which I took as a good sign that we would get along famously.

After the next two women—a nurse and a personal trainer—showed up, we moved outside to enjoy the warm night air. Soon, we were chattering away like we'd known each other for years. None of us had been on Match for more than a couple months and we'd already gone on dates and communicated with a few of the same men. Remember Candy Store Man? Yep, he'd gone out with the lawyer. And the personal trainer and I had both gone out recently with the same man, who had talked incessantly (and bitterly) about his ex-wife.

We drank our wine and chitchatted and then the nurse

informed us that she'd asked a male friend of hers to meet us at the bar. Soon enough, her male friend showed up and the night kind of changed flavor, as they often do when men are around.

After another drink, we all parted ways, promising to get together again. Before the next planned girls' night out, I wrote again to some of the women who'd written me back but hadn't come to the first girls' night out, giving a breezy summation of the night and details for the next meeting spot and time.

And the next time, eight women showed up! (Though the nurse dropped out, never to be seen again. I think the concept of a woman's night out escaped her.) None of the women invited a man to come along and we had a marvelous time comparing our online dating stories.

We started meeting every couple weeks, as we all cycled on and off the dating websites and in and out of various relationships. To say that we were a support for each other would be a vast understatement. It got to the point where if I had a bad date, I'd just think: wait until the girls hear this one.

Online dating can be a lonely experience. It's like you're in your own little bizarro world, like that *Seinfeld* episode where everything was just slightly off-kilter. It's hard to find someone else who understands what you're going through, or who even wants to hear about it. My fellow chefs were only interested in gossiping about each other's food, not my dates. My sister is married to a wonderful man she met in college, and many of my close friends had been married for years.

I think my family and married friends all assumed that I was having the time of my life online dating. I often met married friends or family for dinner, and I usually hadn't taken a sip of wine before someone asked to hear about my latest date. I'd gone to a Rays baseball game and sat in a box? How fun! I'd Googled him afterwards and his mugshot was worse than Nick Nolte's? How hilarious!

The problem is, as anyone who has online dated for more than a day is well aware, online dating can be a bit, um, stressful. Now, I don't mean to be a complainer. It's not like online dating is as stressful as losing a job, or being one of Napoleon's soldiers marching straight into the darkness of a Russian winter, but there is some stress involved, wherever it would fall on a stress measurement meter.

It can be dizzying to fall for yet another smooth player, or to meet a man for coffee or a drink who seems strange or a little off. It's tiring to go through all the mini-breakups and even to craft the graceful emails needed to decline a second or third date and leave a man's ego intact.

It's dispiriting to meet a man who has clearly lied about something quite major. And some dates and relationships go really badly. I don't know about anyone else's health insurance, but my bare-bones individual health insurance doesn't cover mental health care. Since I'd rather spend one hundred and fifty dollars on a funky new pair of sandals or another pair of Joe's Jeans, going to a psychologist is out for me. The wonderful consequence of my contacting other women on Match was that I no longer felt like I needed a therapist. (Usually.) I had my friends to laugh with and to listen to my latest online adventure, and me to theirs.

So how did my girlfriends' relationships go, you might ask? Did my girlfriends have some bad dates along the way, too?

Um, is there a glorious sunrise over Sarasota Bay each morning? That would be a yes—hell to the yes. My girlfriends had some bad dates, too.

One of my new girlfriends showed up at a restaurant to meet a date and was standing idly chatting with the two female greeters at the front desk when a man entered the restaurant wearing a pirate's costume that would have made Jack Sparrow proud, complete with bandana and boots.

She said that one of the women at the front desk whispered to her, "Run! We'll hold him off."

My kind-hearted girlfriend ate lunch with the ersatz pirate and discovered that since she'd recently moved to Florida from a Caribbean island, he'd thought his pirate outfit would make her feel at home. (Uh, no.)

My girlfriends each handled their online dating experiences in slightly different ways. One would get on a dating site for a couple weeks, go on a few bad dates, and then throw in the towel with disgust. Then she'd get back on a month later and do the same thing again. Most of us tried several dating websites, for varying periods of time. One resolutely kept her photo up for two years, setting some sort of world record in dating perseverance, before finding a great relationship offline when a work friend set her up.

Did our group of girlfriends ever hear from or date any of the same men? Absolutely. Sometimes we'd all receive the same mass email. One very desirable man was emailing two of my girlfriends and then asked both for more pictures, by which he clearly meant more revealing photos. One made the mistake of pointing out that the online dating website wasn't an escort service, which earned her quite an ugly email back.

If one of us had a date with a man with unrepresentative photos or other obvious issues, the others knew to stay away. Conversely, if we met a nice man who wasn't a good fit for us, we could recommend him to the others. For instance, I met a marathoner for coffee who wasn't a good fit, but I enthusiastically recommended him to another girlfriend. (And they dated for a short period of time, until he dumped her for a woman ten years younger.)

At a certain point, a couple of us started suggesting to men that we bring a girlfriend along on a first date, if that was all right with them. (It always was.) Even if the date wasn't a good match, it was always fun to have a girlfriend along.

One of my new girlfriends agreed to have a man from a nearby city drive to her condo and spend the afternoon enjoying the beach. They'd happily watched the waves and basked in the sun and then they'd gone back to her condo to change for dinner. They stepped out onto her balcony (which overlooked another condo in the same complex), and he whipped out his you-know-what. As she stared at him—and it—in horror, he said, "Whatsa matter? It's just a cock."

She got him safely back inside and sent him on his way, pleading sudden illness, but she said her neighbors never did seem quite as friendly. She said even as she shut the door behind him she thought about how much we'd enjoy the story. (We did.)

Another one of my girlfriends, a lawyer, began a very promising relationship with a man who shared her passion for yoga. He invited her on a trip to Sedona, Arizona, to some sort of spiritual spa where they would meditate together and absorb Sedona's New-Agey vibe. One night, they got into a very mild argument and the next day he dumped her at the Flagstaff Airport to catch a prop plane to Phoenix and then home, on her own dime. I still remember the confused, sobbing phone call from the airport she'd been unceremoniously dropped off in.

Months later, I was having coffee with the personal trainer and she mentioned a nice man she'd met for a drink the night before. I listened to her describe his work history and his deep interest in yoga and spirituality and I stopped her and asked his name. Yep, it was the same man who had dumped our girlfriend on their spiritual retreat. With that valuable piece of information about his poor conflict-resolution skills, my girlfriend dodged that bullet, unscathed.

When I told one man I met online about my group of girlfriends, he groaned and summed it up perfectly, "You're unionizing!"

When I'm out with a girlfriend and we tell people how we met, we get some odd looks, but just like that woman on *Orange is the New Black*, you never know where you're going to make some new good friends.

16

True Confessions

Remember Elf Sex Man? From the first chapter? He was the man who helpfully sent me a link to a website extolling sex with Icelandic Elves and their "shimmering semen."

A short time after he sent that video, he informed me that he was driving from where he lived in Naples, Florida to Sarasota for a business meeting, and asked if I could meet him for dinner. After a bit of thought, I agreed to meet. What can I say? Is that any more embarrassing than any of the other online dating stories I've told?

And then I started dating him. Again, what can I say? In the negative column, he had sent me a video in which a blonde woman talked enthusiastically about sex with elves. On the plus side, he didn't order for me at dinner and then eat his food and mine, like one of my past dates. He didn't enthusiastically describe the enemas given at his favorite ashram, like yet another. He wasn't living with someone else in another city. He hadn't slept with 300 women, or threatened to throw me over the side of a boat. And… he was exactly my age!

I became quite fond of him. He was sort of a quirky intellectual, and he could always think of something fun to do. I actually allowed myself to hope for a future with him.

Elf Sex Man had a busy life, but we got together as often

as he could. He liked funky road trips—just like me!—and I finally got to see Key West and drink at Hemingway's favorite bar. We ate baskets of fried gator in Everglade City.

One of my ruthlessly pragmatic girlfriends was a bit worried that he was seeing someone else but I asked him and he said he wasn't so I decided to trust.

My mom had been having some strange medical symptoms and was diagnosed with brain cancer, with only a couple weeks to live. Elf Sex Man took this opportunity to slip away into the night, never to be heard from again. He just… disappeared. He never even bothered to break up with me.

So what did I get out of all my time in the online dating world, you might ask? Some wonderful girlfriends, and a lot of vanilla lattes. And I did figure out one better use of my time: writing this book. (And Mom, thanks for listening patiently to all my stories. You are greatly missed.)

To My Dear Readers

I *get* just how frustrating online dating can be. And how time-consuming, heart breaking, and sometimes humiliating, to boot. I get it to the bottom of my pink-painted toenails. After researching online dating, I wanted to shout it from the rooftops to the women trudging through the online dating world: *It's not you, it's online dating!*

The academicians who have studied online dating are clear: make sure to balance online dating with other ways of meeting men. It's a time-consuming process, without great odds of success.

My advice? Find some humor in it all. I know I did.

I wish you the best in finding love, from the bottom of my jaded heart.

Notes

CHAPTER 1

Quotation from Karen Blixen: Hannah Arendt, *The Human Condition* (New York: Doubleday Anchor Books, 1959).

Quotation from Albert Einstein: *Brainyquotes*, http://www.brainyquote.com/quotes/quotes/a/alberteins133991.html

Icelandic elf sex video: interview with Hallgerdur Hallgrímsdóttir, "Icelandic Elf Sex," *Vice*, http://www.vice.com/video/icelandic-elf-sex.

CHAPTER 2

Quotation from Leo Tolstoy: Leo Tolstoy, *The Kreutzer Sonata* 1889. (West Valley City, UT: Waking Lion Press 2006).

Studies that found men prefer physical attractiveness while online dating: Günter Hitsch, Ali Hortaçsu, and Dan Ariely, "What makes you click?—Mate preferences in online dating," *Quantitative Marketing and Economics* 8 (4) (2010): 393-42; Andrew Fiore, "Romantic Regressions: An Analysis of behavior in online dating systems," *Masters Thesis* (Massachusetts Institute of Technology, Cambridge, MA, 2004); Lindsay Shaw Taylor, Andrew Fiore, G.A. Mendelsohn, and Coye Cheshire,

L.V. Krause
"Out of My League," *Personality and Social Psychology Bulletin* 37 (7) (2011): 942-954; and Sheyna Sears-Roberts Alterovitz, G.A. Mendelsohn, "Partner preferences across the life span: Online dating by older adults," *Psychology of Popular Media Culture* 1(S) (2011): 89-95.

Study that analyzed online daters' behavior using binary variables and linear probability models: Günter Hitsch, Ali Hortaçsu, and Dan Ariely, "Matching and Sorting in Online Dating," *American Economic Review* 100(1) (2010): 130-63.

California digital firm attached eye trackers to laptops: http://www.tobii.com/eye-tracking-research/global/library/customer-cases/usability-hci/answerlab/.

Study that found men spend more time browsing profiles than women: Hitsch et al. (2010a).

History of OkCupid: "OkCupid," *Wikipedia*, http://en.wikipedia.org/wiki/OkCupid.

Studies analyzing OkCupid's data, female beauty, and messaging frequency: Christian Rudder, "Your Looks and Your Inbox," OkCupid blog, Nov. 17, 2009, http://blog.okcupid.com/index.php/your-looks-and-online-dating/; and "Mathematics of Beauty," OkCupid blog, January 10, 2011 at http://blog.okcupid.com/index.php/the-mathematics-of-beauty/.

Analysis of Christian Rudder's use of OkCupid user data in *Dataclysm: Who We Are (When We Think No One's Look-*

ing): Evan Selinger, "OkCupid's XOXO for Big Surveillance," *Los Angeles Review of Books*, Oct. 29, 2014, www.lareviewofbooks.org/review/okcupids-xoxo-big-surveillance

Dataclysm sale price information: Logan Hill, "Meet the 4 Most Desired People in New York (According to OKCupid)," *New York Magazine*, Feb. 23, 2014, http://nymag.com/thecut/2014/02/okcupid-most-desired-people-in-newyork.html.

Study analyzing the importance of profile text on OkCupid: Christian Rudder, "We Experiment on Human Beings!" OkCupid blog, July 28, 2014,
http://blog.okcupid.com/index.php/we-experiment-on-human-beings/.

Information about OkCupid's new attractiveness filtering options: Andy Soltis, "Now OkCupid lets you filter out plussize dates," *New York Post*, Oct. 2, 2013,
http://nypost.com/2013/10/02/okcupid-gives-payingusers-a-no-fatties-option/.

Nickname for 'fat' and 'ugly' filter: Amanda Hess, "OkCupid's 'Fat' and 'Ugly' filter won't help you meet your Match," *Slate*, Oct. 3, 2103.

Study using OkCupid data about hot women and frequency of received messages: Christian Rudder, "The Mathematics of Beauty," OkCupid blog, Jan. 10, 2011, http://blog.okcupid.com/index.php/the-mathematics-of-beauty/.

Information about number of words in the English language: *Global Language Monitor*,
http://www.languagemonitor.com/number-of-words/number-of-words-in-the-english-language-1008879/.

The "worst online dating profile ever" experiment: Alli Reed, "Four Things I Learned from the Worst Online Dating Profile Ever," *Cracked*, Jan. 4, 2104, http://www.cracked.com/blog/4-things-i-learned-from-worst-online-dating-profile-ever/#ixzz2pewrAKq2.

Study that found men preferred women with a low BMI: Hitsch et al. (2010b).

Video of Dan Ariely discussing online dating men's BMI preferences: interviewed by David Hirschman "Why Online Dating is so Unsatisfying," *BigThink*, June 1, 2010, http://bigthink.com/videos/why-online-dating-is-so-unsatisfying.

CHAPTER 3

Quotation from Aesop: http://quotes.dictionary.com/Appearances_often_are_deceiving.

Video of Dan Ariely discussing his fellow professor's miserable time online dating: *BigThink* interview (2010).

Study theorizing that online daters are experience goods: Jeana Frost, Zoë Chance, Michael Norton, and Dan Ariely, "People are experience goods: Improving online dating with virtual dates," *Journal of Interactive Marketing* 22 (1) (2008): 51–61.

Two researchers suggest, tentatively, that adding videocams might add to online dating's effectiveness: Eli Finkel and Susan Sprecher, "The Scientific Flaws of Online Dating Sites: What the 'matching algorithms' miss," *Scientific American*, May 8, 2012,
http://www.scientificamerican.com/article/scientific-flaws-online-dating-sites/

CHAPTER 4

Quotation from Tolstoy: Tolstoy, *Anna Karenina* 1877 (London: Penguin Classics Hardcover, 2014).

Study that found men viewed women as less attractive after viewing *Charlie's Angels*: Douglas Kenrick and Sarah Gutierres, "Contrast effects and judgments of physical attractiveness: When beauty becomes a social problems," *Journal of Personality and Social Psychology* 38 (1980): 131-140.

Kenrick analyzed his own *Charlie's Angels* study: Douglas Kenrick, *Sex, Murder, and the Meaning of Life: A Psychologist Investigates How Evolution, Cognition, and Complexity are*

L.V. Krause

Revolutionizing Our View of Human Nature (New York: Basic Books, 2011).

Study that found men viewed women as less attractive after viewing *Playboy* and *Penthouse*: Douglas Kenrick, Sarah Gutierres, and Laurie Goldberg, "Influence of popular erotica on judgments of strangers and mates," *Journal of Experimental Social Psychology* 25 (1989): 159-167.

Study that theorized that looking at beautiful women undermined the average man's satisfaction with average woman: Jon Maner, Douglas Kenrick, D. Vaughn Becker, Andrew Delton, Brian Hofer, Christopher Wilbur, and Steven Neuberg, "Sexually Selective Cognition: Beauty Captures the Mind of the Beholder," *Journal of Personality and Social Psychology* 85(6) (2003) 1107-1120.

Study that found men aren't influenced by their own attractiveness when online messaging: Leonard Lee, George Loewenstein, Dan Ariely, James Hong, and Jim Young, "If I'm not hot, are you hot or not: Physical attractiveness evaluation and dating preferences as a function of one's own attractiveness," *Psychological Science*, 19 (2008): 669–677.

Study that found men are less influenced by their desirability than women while speed dating: Alison Lenton, Barbara Fasolo, and Peter Todd, "'Shopping' for a mate: Expected vs. experienced preferences in online mate choice," *IEEE Transactions on Professional Communication, Special Section: Dar-*

The Real Shark's Tank

winian Perspectives on Electronic Communication 51 (2008):
169-182.

Study that found physical attractiveness was more important to online daters than to those offline: Larry Rosen, Nancy Cheever, Cheyenne Cummings, and Julie Felt, "The Impact of Emotionality and Self-Disclosure on Online Dating versus Traditional Dating," *Computers in Human Behavior* 24 (5) (2008): 2124–2157.

Study analyzing OkCupid's data, female beauty and messaging frequency: Christian Rudder, "Your Looks and Your Inbox," OkCupid blog, Nov. 17, 2009, http://blog.okcupid.com/index.php/your-looks-and-online-dating/.

Studies discussing online daters switching to an assessment mentality: Eli Finkel, Paul Eastwick, Benjamin Karney, Harry Reis, and Susan Sprecher, "Online dating: A critical analysis from the perspective of psychological science," *Psychological Science in the Public Interest*, 13 (2012): 3-66; Becky Heino, Nicole Ellison, and Jennifer Gibbs, "Relationshopping: Investigating the market metaphor in online dating," *Journal of Social and Personal Relationships* 27 (2010): 427–447.

Dan Ariely quotation: *BigThink* interview (2010).

Influential study of online dating: Finkel et al. (2012).

Study that found 64 choices made online daters cognitively

more confused: Alison Lenton, Lars Penke, Peter Todd, and Barbara Fasolo, "The heart has its reasons: Social rationality in mate choice," In R. Hertwig, U. Hoffrage, & the ABC Research Group (Eds.), *Simple heuristics in a social world* (New York: Oxford University Press, 2013). 433-458.

Study that examined human's processing capacities for choice: Lenton, et al. (2008).

Study that discusses mate choice confusion among black grouse and frogs: John Hutchinson, "Is more choice always desirable? Evidence and arguments from leks, food selection, and environmental enrichment," *Biological Reviews of the Cambridge Philosophical Society* 80 (1) (2005): 73-92.

CHAPTER 5

Charts for *The Bachelor* and *The Bachelorette* about their choices: "*The Bachelor* (U.S. TV series)" and "*The Bachelorette*," *Wikipedia*,
   http://en.wikipedia.org/wiki/
The_Bachelor_%28U.S._TV_series%29   and
http://en.wikipedia.org/wiki/The_Bachelorette.

Meredith's alcoholism: Aili Nahas,"*The Bachelorette*'s Meredith Phillips: My Battle with Alcoholism," *People Magazine*, June 3, 2013, http://www.people.com/people/archive/article/0,,20705009,00.html.

Message boards about *The Bachelor* and *The Bachelorette*

seasons: now-archived *TelevisionWithoutPity*, available at
http://web.archive.org/web/20140407043601/
http://forums.televisionwithoutpity.com/forum/997-the-
bachelor-general-gabbery/; and *RealitySteve*,
http://realitysteve.com/.

CHAPTER 6

Study that discusses online daters referring to online dating
in economic terms: Heino et al. (2010).

Background about maximizers and satisficers, including
quiz questions: Barry Schwartz, *The Paradox of Choice* (New
York: Ecco Press 2003).

Study that found maximizers make worse love choices for
themselves online: Mu-Li Yang and Wen-Bin Chiou, "Looking Online for the Best Romantic Partner Reduces Decision
Quality: The Moderating Role of Choice-Making Strategies,"
Cyberpsychology, Behavior, and Social Networking Apr 2010,
13, (2): 207-210.

Study that found maximizers are more prone to depression
and regret: Barry Schwartz, Andrew Ward, John Monterosso,
Sonja Lyubomirsky, Katherine White, and Darrin Lehman,
"Maximizing Versus Satisficing: Happiness Is a Matter of
Choice," *Journal of Personality and Social Psychology* 83(5)
(2002): 1178-1197.

CHAPTER 7

Percentage of male versus female daters on OkCupid, as of Aug. 15, 2015
https://selfserve.rubiconproject.com/advertise3/27503.

Percentage of male versus female daters on Match, as of Aug. 15, 2015:
https://selfserve.rubiconproject.com/advertise3/26935.

Percentage of male versus female daters on OurTime, as of Aug. 15, 2015:
https://selfserve.rubiconproject.com/advertise3/27589.

Percentage of male versus female daters on Chemistry, as of May 15, 2015:
https://selfserve.rubiconproject.com/advertise3/27496.

Percentage of male versus female daters on BlackPeople-Meet, as of Aug.15, 2015:
https://selfserve.rubiconproject.com/advertise3/27592.

Percentage of male versus female daters on eHarmony: Alex Mindlin, "On Niche Dating Sites, Many More Women," *New York Times*, February 26, 2007, http://www.nytimes.com/2007/02/26/technology/26drill.html?_r=0.

Dan Slater's discussion of online dating; quotations from Greg Blatt and Neil Beiderman: Dan Slater, *Love in the Time of Algorithms: What Technology Does to Meeting and Mating* (New York: Current 2013).

Reports that there were significantly more male subscribers to Ashley Madison than women: Julia Greenberg, "Ashley Madison Hack Exposes (Wait For It) A Lousy Business," *Wired*, August 21, 2015, http://www.wired.com/2015/08/ashley-madison-hack-exposes-wait-lousy-business/; Naomi Schaefer Riley, "Ashley Madison Proves Women Aren't Interested in Casual Sex," *New York Post*, August 22, 2015, http://nypost.com/2015/08/22/ashley-madison-proves-women-arent-interested-in-casual-sex/.

Information that many of the female Ashley Madison profiles may have been fake or inactive: Bianca Seidman, "Report: Women's Accounts on Ashley Madison Were Fake," *CBS.com*, August 28, 2015, http://www.cbsnews.com/news/ashley-madison-women-accounts-were-fake-report-says/.

Quotations from Jean-Claude Kaufmann, and his worries about online dating: Jean-Claude Kaufmann, *Love Online* (Cambridge: Polity 2012).

Quotations from Alain Badiou, and his ideas of romance: Alain Badiou, *In Praise of Love* (New York: New Press 2012).

Meetic's status as Europe's largest online dating company: "Meetic," *Wikipedia*, http://en.wikipedia.org/wiki/Meetic.

Analysis of marriages and relationships that started online versus off: Aditi Paul, "Is Online Better Than Offline for Meeting Partners? Depends: Are You Looking to Marry or to

Date?", *Cyberpsychology, Behavior, and Social Networking* 17 (10) (2014): 664-667.

Study of men's and women's different commitment responses when faced with alternatives: John Lydon, "How to Forego Forbidden Fruit: The Regulation of Attractive Alternatives as a Commitment Mechanism," *Social and Personality Psychology Compass* 4 (2010): 635–644.

Study that discusses the problem of high attentiveness to alternatives in a relationship: Rowland Miller, "Inattentive and contented: Relationship commitment and attention to alternatives," *Journal of Personality and Social Psychology*, 73 (1997): 758-766.

Linkage between beer and early civilization: Kurt Stoppkotte, "Beer Brewing Paralleled the Rise of Civilization," April 21, 2001, http://news.nationalgeographic.com/news/2001/04/0424_kurtbeer.html.

CHAPTER 8

Quotation from Greg Behrendt and Liz Tuccillo: Greg Behrendt and Liz Tuccillo, "He's Just Not That Into You: The No-Excuses Truth to Understanding Guys" (New York: Simon Spotlight Entertainment, 2004).

Studies discussing women's desire for more emotional intimacy in casual sexual relationships: Peter Jonason, Norman Li, and Margaret Cason, "The "booty-call": A compromise between men and women's ideal mating strategies," *Journal of Sex Research* 46 (2009): 1-11; Kristen McGinty, David Knox, and Marty Zusman, "Friends with benefits: Women want "'friends', men want 'benefits'," *College Student Journal* 41(4) (2007): 1128-1131.

Study that found 69 percent of women in a friends with benefits relationship hoped the relationship would develop but 60 percent of the men didn't: Justin Lehmiller, Laura VanderDrift, and Janice Kelly, "Sex differences in approaching friends with benefits relationships," *The Journal of Sex Research* 48 (2011): 275-284.

Study discussing women's feeling after casual sex: John Townsend, "Sex without emotional involvement: An evolutionary interpretation of sex differences," *Archives of Sexual Behavior* 24 (1995): 173–206.

Study that discusses women's higher negative feelings after casual sex: Jesse Owen, Galena Rhoades, Scott Stanley, and Frank Fincham, "'Hooking up' among college students: demographic and psychosocial correlates," *Archives of Sexual Behavior*, 39 (3) (2010): 653-63.

Study of women's distress after casual sex: Gary Gute and Elaine Eshbaugh, "Hookups and sexual regret among college women," *Journal of Social Psychology* 148 (2008): 77-89.

Study that found significant differences in men's and women's consent to a suggested casual sexual encounter: Russell Clark and Elaine Hatfield, "Gender differences in receptivity to sexual offers," *Journal of Psychology & Human Sexuality* 2 (1) (1989): 39-55.

Data analysis of single women on OkCupid's desire for casual sex: *Dataclysm: Who We Are (When We Think No One's Looking)* (New York: Crown, 2014).

Quotation from Marcus Frind, and information that he removed the 'intimate encounters' category from POF: Elizabeth Denham, "Interview With Markus Frind, Founder and CEO of Plenty of Fish," *Huffington Post,* June 6, 2013, http://www.huffingtonpost.com/elizabeth-denham/plenty-of-fish-age-difference_b_3381808.html.

Study that originated the term Dark Triad: Delroy Paulhus and Kevin Williams, "The Dark Triad of personality: narcissism, Machiavellianism, and psychopathy," *Journal of Research in Personality* 36 (6) (2002): 556–63.

Studies that discuss the Dark Triad's preference for short-term relationships: Peter Jonason, Norman Li, and David Buss, "The costs and benefits of the Dark Triad: Implications for mate poaching and mate retention tactics," *Personality and Individual Differences* 48 (2010): 373-378; Peter Jonason, Norman Li, Gregory Webster, and David Schmitt, "The dark triad: Facilitating a short-term mating strategy in men," *European Journal of Personality,* 23 (2009): 5–18.

Studies that found significantly higher levels of Dark Triad traits in men than women: Peter Jonason, Serena Wee, Norman Li, and Christopher Jackson, "Occupational niches and the Dark Triad traits," *Personality and Individual Differences* 69 (2014): 119-123; Jonason, Li, Webster and Schmitt (2009); Paulhus and Williams (2002).

Study that links the Dark Triad to internet trolling: Erin Buckels, Paul Trapnell, and David Paulhus, "Trolls Just Want to Have Fun," *Personality and Individual Differences* 67 (2014): 97-102.

Study that links the Dark Triad to bad bosses: Peter Jonason, Sarah Slomski, and Jamie Partyka, "The Dark Triad at work: How toxic employees get their way," *Personality and Individual Differences* 52 (3) (2012): 449–53.

Background on Niccolò Machiavelli: "Niccolò Machiavelli," *Wikipedia*, http://en.wikipedia.org/wiki/Niccolò_Machiavelli.

Study discussing narcissists' craving for attention and admiration: Joshua Foster, Ilan Shrira, and W. Keith Campbell, "Theoretical models of narcissism, sexuality, and relationship commitment," *Journal of Social and Personal Relationships* 23 (3) (2006): 367-386.

Studies discussing psychopaths' tendency toward thrill-seeking, callous behavior: Peter Jonason, Bryan Koenig, and Jeremy Tost, "Living a *fast* life: The Dark Triad and Life History Theory," *Human Nature*, 21 (2010): 428-442; Peter Jonason, Gregory Webster, David Schmitt, Norman Li, and Laura

Crysel, "The antihero in popular culture: A Life History Theory of the Dark Triad," *Review of General Psychology* 16 (2012): 192-199.

Study that discusses high-functioning psychopaths: Peter Jonason, Norman Li, and Emily Teicher, "Who is James Bond?: The Dark Triad as an agentic social style," *Individual Differences Research* 8 (2010): 111–120.

Study that discusses the Dark Triad's game-playing love style: Peter Jonason and Phillip Kavanagh, "The dark side of love: The Dark Triad and love styles," *Personality and Individual Differences* 49 (2010): 606-610.

Study that links personality styles of the Dark Triad to relationship preferences:

Peter Jonason, Victor Luevano, and Heather Adams, "How the Dark Triad traits

predict relationship choices" *Personality and Individual Differences* 53 (2012) 180–184.

Study exploring the Dark Triad's lack of empathy: Peter Jonason, Minna Lyons, Emily Bethell, and Rahael Ross, "Different routes to limited empathy in the sexes: Examining the links between the Dark Triad and empathy," *Personality and Individual Differences* 57 (2013) 572-576.

The 12-point Dark Triad test: Peter Jonason and George Webster, "The dirty dozen: A concise measure of the dark triad," *Psychological Assessment* 22(2) (2010): 420-432.

The Real Shark's Tank

Studies that discuss narcissists' initial good impression fading over time: Mitja Back, Stefan Schmukle, and Boris Egloff, "Why are narcissists so charming at first sight? Decoding the narcissism-popularity link at zero acquaintance," *Journal of Personal Social Psychology* 98 (1) (2010): 132-45; W. Keith Campbell, Craig Foster, and Eli Finkel, "Does self-love lead to love for others?: A story of narcissistic game-playing," *Journal of Personality and Social Psychology* 83 (2002): 340–354.

Studies that discuss narcissists' charm allowing them to easily begin new relationships: Back et al. (2010); Campbell et al. (2002).

Studies that discuss narcissists' lack of desire for emotional intimacy: Campbell and Foster (2007); Campbell et al. (2002).

Study that found narcissists associate certain words like '"power" with sex: Foster et al. (2006).

Discussion of narcissists' perception of their romantic partners and their ex-partners' perception of them: Joshua Foster, "Narcissists Don't Make Love: What do narcissists think of when they think of sex?" *Psychology Today, The Narcissus in All of Us* blog, October 31, 2008,
http://www.psychologytoday.com/blog/the-narcissus-in-all-us/200810/narcissists-dont-make-love.

Study that found narcissists tend to be flirtatious: Campbell et al. (2002).

Study that found narcissists have a tendency to initiate friendships to help with finding a mate: Peter Jonason and David Schmitt, "What have you done for me lately?: Friendship-selection in the shadows of Dark Triad traits," *Evolutionary Psychology* 10 (2012): 400-421.

Study that describes narcissists' high use of sexual language in a normal context: Nicholas Holtzman, Simine Vazire, and Mattias Mehl, "Sounds like a narcissist: Behavioral manifestations of narcissism in everyday life," *Journal of Research in Personality* 44 (2010): 478-484.

Study that found narcissists have a preference for friends with benefits relationships: Jonason, Luevano, and Adams (2102).

Study that discusses narcissists' tendency to put others down, and their love for material goods: W. Keith Campbell and Joshua Foster, "The Narcissistic Self: Background, an Extended Agency Model, and Ongoing Controversies." In C. Sedikides & S. Spencer (Eds.), *Frontiers in social psychology: The self* (Philadelphia, PA: Psychology Press, 2007). 115-138.

Study that discusses narcissists' high attractiveness levels: Nicholas Holtzman and Michael Strube, "Narcissism and attractiveness," *Journal of Research in Personality* (2010): 133-136.

Study that discusses narcissists' preference for "*trophy romantic partners*": Campbell et al. (2002).

Studies that discuss narcissists' tendency to search for better dating alternatives and to show a lack of commitment: Campbell et al. (2002); and Campbell and Foster (2007).

Study that found narcissists tend to be unfaithful: Campbell et al. (2002).

Study that describes narcissists' tendency to be easily insulted: Daniel Jones and Delroy Paulhus, "Different provocations trigger aggression in narcissists and psychopaths," *Social Psychological and Personality Science* 1 (2010): 12–18.

Studies that discuss narcissists' desire to date people who make them look good: Campbell and Foster (2007); and Campbell et al. (2002).

Studies that discuss narcissists' tendency toward a lack of sexual empathy and coercive sexual behavior: Brad Bushman, Angelica Bonacci, Mirjam van Dijk, and Roy Baumeister, "Narcissism, sexual refusal, and aggression: testing a narcissistic reactance model of sexual coercion," *Journal of Personality and Social Psychology* 84(5) (2003): 1027-40; and Keith Williams, Barry Cooper, Teresa Howell, John Yuille, and Delroy Paulhus, "Inferring sexually deviant behavior from corresponding fantasies: The role of personality and pornography consumption," *Criminal Justice and Behavior*, 36 (2009): 130-137.

Studies describing narcissists' tendency toward relationship intention deception: Jonason, Li, and Buss (2010); and Jonason, Li, Webster, and Schmitt (2009).

Greek mythology, Narcissus's death: "Narcissus (mythology)," *Wikipedia,* en.wikipedia.org/wiki/Narcissus_(mythology).

Study describing Machiavellians' cynicism and their 'ends justify the means' world view: Daniel Jones and Delroy Paulhus, "Machiavellianism." In M. R. Leary & R. H. Hoyle (Eds.), *Handbook of Individual Differences in Social Behavior* (New York: Guilford, 2009) 93-108.

Studies showing association between Machiavellianism and success in stock, real estate, and car sales: Abdul Aziz, Kim May, and John Crotts, "Relations of Machiavellian Behavior with Sales Performance of Stockbrokers," *Psychological Reports* 90 451-460; Abdul Aziz "Relationship between Machiavellianism scores and performance of real estate salespersons," *Psychological Reports* 96 (1) (2010): 235-238; and Abdul Aziz, "Machiavellianism scores and self-rated performance of automobile salespersons," *Psychological Reports,* 94 (2) (2010): 464-466.

Study that associated Machiavellians with love-feigning and a coercive use of intoxication for sex: John McHoskey, "Machiavellianism and sexuality: On the moderating role of biological sex," *Personality and Individual Differences* 31 (2001): 779–789.

Study that discusses Machiavellians' intelligence: Jones and Paulhus (2009).

Studies that discuss Machiavellians' tendency to infidelity in relationships: McHoskey, (2001); and Paulhus and Williams (2002).

Study that discusses Machiavellians' tendency to deceive to get sex: McHoskey (2001).

Studies that describe Machiavellians' tendency to lie about their relationship intentions, involvement, and relationship status: Jonason, Luévano, and Adams (2012); and Peter Jonason, Minna Lyons, Holly Baughman, and Phillip Vernon, "What a tangled web we weave: The Dark Triad and deception," *Personality and Individual Differences* 70, (2014): 117-119.

Study that discusses Machiavellians' self-reports about willingness to cheat in a broad variety of situations: Jones and Paulhus (2009).

Study that found Machiavellians lie about their finances, and lie about their intentions in relationships: Susan Aitken, Minna Lyons, Peter Jonason, "Dads or cads?: Women's strategic decisions in the mating game," *Personality and Individual Differences*, 55 (2013): 118-122.

Study that discusses Machiavellians not choosing helping professions: Andrea Czibor and Tamas Bereczkei, (2012)

"Machiavellian people's success results from monitoring their partners," *Personality and Individual Differences*," 53 (2012).

Study that describes Machiavellians' negative, cynical worldview: Jones and Paulhus (2009).

Study that discusses Machiavellians dark view of human nature, and their reluctance to volunteer unless it benefits them: Ernest O'Boyle, Donelson Forsyth, George Banks, and Michael McDaniel, "Meta-analysis of the Dark Triad and work behavior: A social exchange perspective," *Journal of Applied Psychology* 97 (3) (2012): 557–579.

Study that found psychopaths are found at higher levels in financial service organizations: Clive R.P. Boddy, "Corporate Psychopaths and organizational type," *Journal of Public Affairs* 10 (4) (2010): 300–312.

Studies that discuss psychopaths' interest in casual sex: Jonason, Luevano, and Adams (2012); and Jonason, Koenig, and Tost (2010).

Study that linked an enjoyment of casual sex with no emotional attachment, and a high number of sexual partners to psychopathy: Rebecca Kastner and Martin Sellbom, "Hypersexuality in College Students: the Role of Psychopathy," *Personality and Individual Differences* 53 (5) (2012): 644-649.

Study that found psychopathic males use coercion, alcohol and flattery for sex:

The Real Shark's Tank
David Kosson, Jennifer Kelly, and Jacquelin White "Psychopathy-Related Traits Predict Self-Reported Sexual Aggression Among College Men," *Journal of Interpersonal Violence* 12 (2): (1997) 241-254.

General background, psychopathy: Paul Babiak and Robert Hare, *Snakes in Suits: When Psychopaths Go to Work*, (New York, NY: ReganBooks, 2006); Jon Ronan, *The Psychopath Test: the Journey Through the Madness Industry* (New York, NY: Riverhead Hardcover, 2011).

Study describing psychopaths' tendency toward schaden-freude:
Phillip Kavanagh, Samantha James, Peter Jonason, Jill Chonody, and Hayley Scrutton, "The Dark Triad, schaden-freude, and sensational interests: Dark personality, dark emotions, and dark behaviors," *Personality and Individual Differences* 68 (2014): 211-216.

Studies describing psychopaths' interest in violence and violent media: Kavanaugh, James, Jonason, Chonody, and Scrutton (2014); Kevin Williams, Delroy Paulhus, and Robert Hare, "Capturing the four-factor structure of psychopathy in college students via self-report," *Journal of Personal Assessment* 88 (2) (2007): 205-19.

Study that linked psychopaths to booty calls: Jonason, Luevano, and Adams (2012).

Study that linked psychopaths to poorer relationships with

parents and children, alcohol and drug use, and other risk-taking activities: Jonason, Koenig, and Tost (2010).

Studies that discuss psychopaths' tendency toward infidelity: Jonason, Li and Buss (2010); Jonason, Li, Webster, and Schmitt (2009); Heather Adams, Victor Luévano, and Peter Jonason, "Risky business: Willingness to be caught in an extra-pair relationship, relationship experience, and the Dark Triad," *Personality and Individual Differences* 66, 204-207.

CHAPTER 9

Discussion on subreddit message board 2XChromosomes by a man pretending to be a female on OkCupid, and two representive comments following his post: http://www.reddit.com/r/TwoXChromosomes/comments/1uqym6/as_a_guy_i_wanted_to_know_what_it_was_like_to_be/.

Information that Markus Frind removed the ability of male members to send photos to female members: Elizabeth Denham, "Interview With Markus Frind, Founder and CEO of Plenty of Fish," *Huffington Post*, June 6, 2013, http://www.huffingtonpost.com/elizabeth-denham/plenty-of-fish-age-difference_b_3381808.html.

Article about the 4 most popular users of OkCupid in 4 different categories in NYC: Logan Hill, "Meet the 4 Most Desired People in New York (According to OKCupid)," *New*

The Real Shark's Tank
York Magazine, Feb. 23, 2014, http://nymag.com/thecut/2014/02/okcupid-most-desired-people-in-new-york.html.

Study that discusses people's improved behavior online if they have mutual acquaintances: Judith Donath and Danah Boyd, "Public Displays of Connection," *Bt Technology Journal*, 22 (4) (2004): 71-82.

Study describing disinhibition: John Suler, "The Online Disinhibition Effect," *CyberPsychology & Behavior* 7 (3) (2004): 321-6.

CHAPTER 10

IAC corporate website information about Japanese Match.com identity verification option: Press release, Oct. 24, 2008, http://iac.com/media-room/press-releases/matchcom-japan-extends-leadership-position-online-dating-serving-nearly-1.

Book by Stanford business professor about his online dating: Paul Oyer, *Everything I Ever Needed to Know About Economics I Learned From Online Dating* (Boston: Harvard Business Review Press, 2013.)

Article about identity verification on Asian online dating sites: Paul Oyer, "How Asian Dating sites cracked your biggest complaint—everyone lies online," *Quartz*, January 17, 2014, http://qz.com/167879/how-asian-dating-sites-cracked-your-biggest-complaint-everyone-lies-online/.

Match group division revenue: IAC 10-K annual report, filed on Feb. 27, 2015, http://ir.iac.com/secfiling.cfm?filingID=891103-15-4&CIK=891103.

Study that described amount of lying on dating sites: Jeffrey Hancock, Catalina Toma, and Nicole Ellison, "The truth about lying on online dating profiles," *CHI 2007 Proceedings*, (2007): 449-452.

Study that found online daters were "somewhat creative": Whitty, M. "Revealing the 'real' me, searching for the 'actual' you: Presentations of self on an internet dating site" *Computers in Human Behavior*" 24 (2008): 1707–1723.

Study that found women more likely to post old photos, and retouched or professional photos: Jeffrey Hancock, and Catalina Toma, "Putting Your Best Face Forward: The Accuracy of Online Dating Photographs," *Journal of Communication*, 59 (2009): 367–386.

Study that found women more likely to lie about weight: Hancock et al. (2007).

Studies that found men more likely to lie about relationship status: Catalina Toma, Jeffrey Hancock, and Nicole Ellison, "Separating Fact from Fiction: An Examination of Deceptive Self-Presentation in Online Dating Profiles," *Personality and Social Psychology Bulletin*, 34 (8) (2008): 1023–1036; and Whitty (2008).

The Real Shark's Tank

Study that found men more likely to lie about attributes, interests, assets, goals, and age: Jeffrey Hall, Namkee Park, Hayeon Song, and Michael Cody, "Strategic misrepresentation in online dating: The effects of gender, self-monitoring, and personality traits," *Journal of Social and Personal Relationships*, 27 (1) (2010): 117-135.

Study that found men lie more often, lie to more people, and also think they're better liars than women: Jonason, Lyons, Baughman, and Vernon (2014).

Study that found men are more likely to lie to achieve short-term goals with women: Catalina Toma, Jeffrey Hancock, and Nicole Ellison, "Separating Fact from Fiction: An Examination of Deceptive Self-Presentation in Online Dating Profiles," *Personality and Social Psychology Bulletin*, 34 (8) (2008): 1023–1036.

Statistic about number of fake or scammer profiles on dating sites: Robert L. Mitchell, "Online dating: the technology behind the attraction,"
Computerworld, November 13, 2009,
http://www.itworld.com/article/2770281/networking-hardware/online-dating–the-technology-behind-the-attraction.html.

Statistics on internet romance scams: 2013 Internet Crime Report, Internet Crime Report Center, https://www.ic3.gov/media/annualreport/2013_IC3Report.pdf.

L.V. Krause

Romantic scam advice from the FBI: http://www.fbi.gov/ news/stories/2012/february/dating-scams_021412/dating-scams_021412.

Press release from the U.S. Army warning about romance scammers: United States Army Criminal Investigation Command, "U.S. Army CID Pleads with Public, Warns Against Romance Scams," Oct. 17, 2011, http://www.cid.army.mil/ documents/RomanceScamsOct11.pdf.

Information that an army officer whose photos were stolen was contacted by 300 scammed women: Joe Gould, "Army says romance scammers using soldiers' pics," *Army Times*, Dec. 5, 2010, http://archive.armytimes.com/article/20121205/ NEWS/212050316/Army-says-romance-scammers-using-soldiers-pics.

CHAPTER 11

Quotation from Brian Bowman: Dan Slater, *Love in the Time of Algorithms: What Technology Does to Meeting and Mating.* (New York: Current 2013).

Definition "Algorithm": *Wikipedia*, https://en.wikipedia.org/wiki/Algorithm.

Quotation from Brian Bowman: Dan Slater, *Love in the Time of Algorithms: What Technology Does to Meeting and Mating.* (New York: Current 2013).

PlentyOfFish to be bought by the Match Group: Georgia Wells and Angela Chen, "IAC's Match Plans a New Hookup," July 14, 2015, *Wall Street Journal*, http://www.wsj.com/articles/match-group-to-buy-dating-site-plentyoffish-for-575-million-1436877537.

Information about POF matching: POF website, http://www.pof.com/suggestions_v2.aspx?section=9.

Quotation from Christian Rudder: Andrew Leonard, "OkCupid founder: 'I wish people exercised more humanity' on OkCupid," *Salon*, Sept. 12, 2014.

Helen Fisher's quotation, her recruitment to Chemistry.com, information about Chemistry.com's matching system: Rebecca Traister, "Cupid's Science" *Salon*, Aug. 20, 2007, http://www.salon.com/2007/08/20/chemistry/; Joseph Hooper, The Laws of Attraction," *Elle*, Jan. 13, 2009, http://www.elle.com/life-love/sex-relationships/advice/a9020/the-laws-of-attraction-284520/.

Background, Neil Clark Warren: "Neil Clark Warren," *Wikipedia*, http://en.wikipedia.org/wiki/Neil_Clark_Warren.

Quotation from eHarmony beginning *"Out of all the single people you will meet in your life... "*: can be retrieved at http://www.eharmony.com/why/science-of-compatibility/.

Eharmony, 29 Dimensions® of Personality: can be retrieved

at http://www.eharmony.com/why/dating-relationship-compatibility/.

John Tierney's eHarmony experiment: John Tierney, "My eHarmony Experiment: Can This Marriage Be Matched?", *NYTimes,* Feb. 1, 2009, Tierneylab.blogs.nytimes.com/2008/ 02/01/my-eharmony-experiment-can-this-marriage-be-matched/comment-page-5/?_r=0.

Quotation from Eli Finkel: Nick Bolton, "Tinder, the Fast-Growing Dating App, Taps an Age-Old Truth," *New York Times,* Oct. 30, 2014, http://www.nytimes.com/2014/10/30/ fashion/tinder-the-fast-growing-dating-app-taps-an-age-old-truth.html.

Quotations from Thomas Bradbury and Benjamin Karney: Amanda Lewis, "UCLA Professors Say eHarmony is Unscientific and Its Customers Are Duped. Here's Why," *LAWeekly,* April 16, 2012, http://www.laweekly.com/arts/ucla-professors-say-eharmony-is-unscientific-and-its-customers-are-duped-heres-why-2370923.

Calls for more rigorous proof of dating companies matching formulas discussed: Finkel et al. (2012).

Study that pooled 313 other studies assessing similarity and relationship satisfaction: R. Mathew Montoya, Robert Horton, and Jeffrey Kirchner, "Is actual similarity necessary for attraction? A meta-analysis of actual and perceived similarity," *Journal of Social and Personal Relationships* 25 (2008): 889–922.

Study that discusses relationship satisfaction causes: Finkel et al. (2012).

Quotation from Robert Epstein: Robert Epstein, "The Truth about Online Dating," *Scientific American*, Feb/March 2007, http://www.scientificamerican.com/article/the-truth-about-online-da/.

CHAPTER 12

Quotation by Leonore Coffee: http://www.quotehd.com/ quotes/lenore-coffee-quote-when-a-man-of-forty-falls-in-love-with-a-girl-of-twenty-it.

Christie Brinkley feels invisible to men her age: ETonline staff, "Brinkley opens up about dating younger men," *Entertainment Tonight*, Jan. 29, 2014.

Study describing online dating users' using limited searching criteria: Heino et al. (2010).

Quotation and data about men's messaging rates to same-aged women: Christian Rudder, *Dataclysm: Who We Are (When We Think No One's Looking)* (New York: Crown, 2014.)

Information that Markus Frind decreed that POF members outside of a 14-year age range could not contact each other: Yvonne Mazzulo, "Plenty of Fish dating site removes 'Intimate Encounters' option," *The Examiner*, May 21, 2013,

L.V. Krause
http://www.examiner.com/article/plenty-of-fish-dating-site-removes-intimate-encounters-option.

Quotation from Evan Marc Katz: Evan Marc Katz, "Am I Too Old to Have Success in Online Dating?", http://www.evanmarckatz.com/blog/online-dating-tips-advice/am-i-too-old-to-have-success-in-online-dating/.

Information about singles over 50 being fastest growing group of online daters: quotation from Sam Yagan, CEO of Match.group, by Ina Jaffe, "ISO Romance: Dating Sites Help Older Singles," *NPR*, Feb. 25, 2014, http://www.npr.org/blogs/alltechconsidered/2014/02/25/282589142/iso-romance-dating-sites-help-older-singles.

Study describing older men's preference for even younger women: Jens Asenforpf, Lars Penke, and Mitja Back, "From dating to mating and relating: Predictors of initial and long-term outcomes of speed-dating in a community sample," *European Journal of Personality*, 25 (1) (2011) 16-30.

Study that found men in fifties prefer much younger women: Douglas Kenrick and Richard Keefe, "Age preferences in mates reflect sex differences in human reproductive strategies," *Behavioral and Brain Science*, 15 (1) (1992): 75-91.

CHAPTER 13

Amount of money spent for online dating advertising in the first five months of 2014: Nathalie Tadena, "What

Match.com's Ad Spending Says About Online Dating," *Wall Street Journal,* June 4, 2104, blogs.wsj.com/cmo/2014/06/04/what-match-coms-ad-spending-says-about-online-dating/.

Match group division revenue: IAC 10-K annual report, filed on Feb. 27, 2015, http: http://ir.iac.com/secfiling.cfm?filingID=891103-15-4&CIK=891103.

Match relationship success statistics: 2014 "Match fact sheet," http://match.mediaroom.com/index.php?s=30440.

Marriage statistics, online dating: Aaron Smith, "5 Facts about online dating," *The Pew Report,* Feb. 13, 2014, http://www.pewresearch.org/fact-tank/2014/02/13/5-facts-about-online-dating/.

Study using OkCupid data to analyze marriage success rates for eHarmony and Match: Christian Rudder, "Why You Should Never Pay For Online Dating," OkCupid blog, April 7, 2010, now deleted, available at http://static.izs.me/why-you-should-never-pay-for-online-dating.html.

Information about OkCupid's sale price: IAC website, Iac.com/about/leadership/business-management/sam-yagan.

Quotation from Sam Yagen about deleted OkCupid blog post: Adrianne Jeffries, "OKCupid: We Didn't Censor Our Match.com-Bashing Blog Post," *New York Observer,* Feb. 2, 2011, http://observer.com/2011/02/okcupid-we-didnt-censor-our-matchcombashing-blog-post/.

Discussion about dating companies' marriage statistics: Carl Bialik, "Marriage-Maker Claims Are Tied in Knots," *Wall Street Journal*, July 29, 2009, http://www.wsj.com/articles/ SB124879877347487253.

The head of Match product comments about inactive profiles: Dan Slater, *Love in the Time of Algorithms* (New York: Current, 2013).

Class action lawsuit against Match.com filed: "*David Robinson, et al v. Match.com, LLC,*" filed 12/30/10, http://www.ndtexblog.com/wpcontent/uploads/2011/01/ 17715463268.pdf.

Class action lawsuit against Match.com decided: "*David Robinson, et al. v. Match.com, LLC,*" decided 8/10/12, http://www.gpo.gov/fdsys/pkg/USCOURTS-txnd-3_10-cv-02651/pdf/USCOURTS-txnd-3_10-cv-02651-0.pdf.

Academics call for Federal Trade Commission regulation of online dating companies: Finkel et al. (2012); Thompson et al. (2005).

Information about the FTC's regulation of consumer goods: http://www.ftc.gov/about-ftc/bureaus-offices/bureau-consumer-protection.

Information about FTC's lawsuit against lingerie companies for promoting cellulite reduction shapewear garments: http://www.ftc.gov/enforcement/cases-proceedings/132-3095/wacoal-america-inc-matter.

FTC guidelines concerning the use of endorsements and testimonials in advertising: http://www.ftc.gov/sites/default/files/attachments/press-releases/ftc-publishes-final-guides-governing-endorsements-testimonials/091005revisedendorsementguides.pdf.

Academic co-authors question whether dating websites are a productive use of time: Finkel et al. (2012).

Advertising industry website: "Match.com TV Commercials," *iSpot.tv*,

http://www.ispot.tv/brands/AoT/match-com

About the Author

L.V. Krause is a Minnesota-born author, thus explaining her excessive politeness with her online dates. She lives in the swampland now called Florida.

Thought Catalog, it's a website.
www.thoughtcatalog.com

Social
facebook.com/thoughtcatalog
twitter.com/thoughtcatalog
tumblr.com/thoughtcatalog
instagram.com/thoughtcatalog

Corporate
www.thought.is

www.ingramcontent.com/pod-product-compliance
Lightning Source LLC
Chambersburg PA
CBHW031532040426
42445CB00010B/504